Best Care Anywhere

Best Care Anywhere

Why VA Health Care Is Better Than Yours

PHILLIP LONGMAN

 PoliPointPress

Best Care Anywhere:
Why VA Health Care Is Better Than Yours

This edition published in the United States of America by PoliPointPress, P.O. Box 3008, Sausalito, CA 94966-3008; www.p3books.com

Production management: BookMatters
Book design: BookMatters
Cover design: Jeff Kenyon

Library of Congress Cataloging-in-Publication Data

Longman, Phillip.

   Best care anywhere : Why VA health care is better than yours / by Phillip Longman. (1956–   )
     p.   cm.
   ISBN-10: 0-9778253-0-2
   1. United States. Dept. of Veterans Affairs.
   2. ∞Veterans—Medical care—United States.
   3. ∞Medical care—United States. I. Title.

UB369.L66   2007
362.1086'970973—dc22   2006032594

Printed in the United States of America
February 2007

Published by:
PoliPointPress, LLC
P.O. Box 3008
Sausalito, CA 94966-3008
(415) 339-4100
www.p3books.com

Distributed by Publishers Group West

Contents

Foreword

Timothy Noah

The most important domestic policy discussion in the United States is one that isn't taking place. The subject is whether socialized medicine, already available to the elderly (through Medicare), to the poor (through Medicaid), and to veterans (through the Veterans Administration) should be extended to the rest of the population. The discussion has yet to begin for two reasons unrelated to the merits of the case.

The first is that the Democratic Party, the logical advocate for nationalizing health care, is still intimidated by the political disaster it suffered the last time it took on the issues. Fairly or not, much of the blame for Democrats' epochal loss of the House in 1994 was heaped on "Hillarycare," the ambitious plan to reform the health care system championed by First Lady (now Senator) Hillary Clinton. Hillarycare was not a scheme for the federal government to start paying everybody's doctor bills, but the plan's perceived complexity frightened Democrats away from considering *any* large-scale changes to the way Americans receive health care.

The second reason nobody's talking about whether and how the federal government should assume financial responsibility for health care is the bipartisan assumption nowadays that the government could never run anything as complex and vital as the health care industry. In the political climate of the past quarter-century, to suggest otherwise has been to remove oneself from the political mainstream. In the meantime, evidence has quietly accumulated that the best medical care available in the United States is also the most purely socialistic.

How government succeeded where capitalism did not is the story related in this rigorously researched and tightly argued book. Its author, Phillip Longman, is one of the country's most gifted economic journalists, skilled to an unusual degree at both shoe-leather reporting and academic research and analysis. He is no free-spending liberal. Longman made his name writing about wasteful government subsidies to the middle class and how they warp the economy. (He once published a book under the title *The Return of Thrift*.) When Longman began the research for the magazine article that led to this book, his initial bias was to blame the high cost and inefficiency of U.S. medical care on government spending. But study after study kept identifying the health care system's locus of quality in veterans hospitals, which are paid for and run by the federal government. Like any good reporter, Longman set aside his preconceptions to follow the facts.

Why are veterans hospitals better than other hospitals? Partly, Longman explains, because they're better able to focus on the long term. Patients shuffle in and out of private health care plans, either because they change jobs or because their employer decides to do business with a different (read: cheaper) insurance company. This is quite different from the Department of Veterans Affairs (VA), which signs up a patient for life, and therefore *saves money* whenever it improves a patient's likelihood of enjoying good health over the long term. Another reason the VA system is superior to private hospitals is that the VA's doctors are salaried and therefore lack any conceivable financial incentive to subject patients to avoidable medical procedures, which are responsible for a great deal of bad health outcomes. The VA's main advantage, however, comes from its having adopted the same modern information technologies embraced by virtually every other sector of the economy—technologies that the health care industry has tended to resist.

Longman's first inkling of what ailed the health care industry came about through personal experience. His wife, Robin, became seriously ill, and the two ended up spending a lot of time inside hospitals. A few years later, I had a similar experience. My wife, Marjorie, was diagnosed with fourth-stage liver cancer. Because we were affluent, and because we had unusually generous and understanding employers, we were able to devote most of our waking hours to Marjorie's medical care.

Much of our effort involved retrieving information from one source and sending it to another. This wasn't something we could count on happening on its own. Very expensive blood test results, we observed, had perhaps a 50 percent chance of being misplaced under a pile of faxes and therefore never finding their way into Marjorie's medical chart. So we made a habit of getting the labs to fax results to our house. Films of CT scans would be misfiled perhaps 30 percent of the time and thus become permanently irretrievable. (Doctors who examined the films were the worst culprits.) So I took my checkbook to all of Marjorie's CT scans and purchased my own spare copy on the spot. Often I would wonder: What happens to people who lack the time, patience, or money to assemble a duplicate data file? Even with all this cajoling and faxing and running to hospital film libraries, we sometimes failed to get our hands on a particular piece of medical information in time for a crucial doctor's appointment. In some of those instances, Marjorie's doctor would end up making medical decisions without having all the relevant data in hand. Marjorie's prognosis was sufficiently hopeless—she died in 2005—that the consequence of any such decision wouldn't likely have affected the outcome. But that logic doesn't hold for most hospital patients.

The inability of information to travel from point A to point B is a problem that computer technology can easily solve, but hospitals have been loath to computerize medical records, in large part because it's difficult for them to recoup such an investment. The benefit, to any individual patient, is straightforward, particularly in preventing and managing long-term conditions like diabetes. But since patients typically switch from one health care plan to another every several years, individual health care providers have little or no financial incentive to invest in electronic medical records and other technologies that will mostly benefit their competitors.

The Bush administration has pushed energetically to provide more information technology in hospitals, but its commitment to making health care more competitive and market driven can only undermine that effort. "Health savings accounts" are a case in point. These are new, tax-free accounts that can be used only to pay medical expenses. But, as Arnold Relman, former editor of the *New England Journal of Medicine*, has observed, the more freedom we give individuals to purchase their own health care financing schemes, the more efficiently the market will punish those in poor health:

> Healthy, young families would choose the least expensive plans with the highest allowable deductible, and those with

health problems would be forced to choose plans with the lowest allowable deductibles but higher premiums. The premiums or the required co-payments of the latter plans would spiral upward because of the greater use of services by sicker beneficiaries, so it would become even harder for those with the greatest need for insurance to afford coverage. In this way, one of the most important values of insurance—the sharing of risks over a broad population base—would be lost.[1]

To whatever extent hospitals absorbed these costs themselves, they'd have even less money left over than they do now to pay for computerization.

A major worry about the government assuming control of health care is that citizens will become insatiable consumers of it, since they won't have to pay for it directly. Many economists think this is already happening today with third-party payment by health insurers encouraging too many vaccinations, too many visits to the dentist, and too many annual checkups (to quote the 2004 *Economic Report to the President*). But as Paul Krugman and Robin Wells observed recently in the *New York Review of Books*, it isn't oral prophylaxis that's driving medical care costs through the roof; it's the health care provided to seriously ill patients.[2] It's people like Robin and Marjorie. "When you think of the problem of health care costs," Krugman and Wells wrote,

> you shouldn't envision visits to the family physician to talk about a sore throat; you should think about coronary bypass operations, dialysis, and chemotherapy. Nobody is proposing a consumer-directed health care plan that would force individuals to pay a large share of extreme medical expenses, such as the costs of chemotherapy, out of pocket.

And that means that consumer-directed health care can't promote savings on the treatments that account for most of what we spend on health care.[3]

What Longman demonstrates in the book you are about to read is that many of the routine doctor visits that market-minded economists see as wasteful (in the short term) bring savings to the health care system (over the long term). We fail to recognize this only because private health insurers and hospitals are—and, structured as they are, must be—entirely indifferent to the long term. What's really needed, then, is to make private hospitals more like VA hospitals. Even President Bush has acknowledged (in his characteristic broken English) that "the VA has got an advantage because the—all the administrators work for the same—same outfit, the same organization." But the president doesn't want to think about what that says about market-based health care. It's about time the rest of us did.

Introduction

Several years ago, *Fortune* magazine summoned me to New York for a sumptuous lunch and a serious discussion. At the end of the meal, I found myself with a plum, but difficult, freelance assignment. It was no less than to figure out who had the best solutions for America's health care crisis, and to write them up in snappy prose that would make the story a "must read" for the country's business elite. What the magazine had in mind, I think, was that I find some dynamic, change-artist CEO who was doing for health care what Andrew Grove had once done for Intel or what Jack Welsh had done for General Electric.

I accepted these marching orders with much trepidation, but also great curiosity and passion. The biggest reason was personal. Five years before, I had lost my wife, Robin, to breast cancer. I never blamed her doctors for her death. But what I saw of the American health care system during the 10 months between her diagnosis and demise had caused me to stop regarding health care as a mere abstraction. I had become personally engaged in the question of how the American health care system actually worked, or all too often, didn't work.

Robin was treated at the prestigious Lombardi Cancer

Center, part of Georgetown University's hospital, in upscale Northwest Washington, D.C. Every time she and I entered the facility through its posh lobby, we passed a poster-sized blow-up, mounted on an easel, of a recent cover of *U.S. News & World Report* that ranked Lombardi as one of the best cancer treatment centers in the country. Since I worked at *U.S. News* at the time and respected the team responsible for these annual rankings, this was particularly reassuring.

Robin and I both felt blessed that our gold-plate insurance allowed us unfettered access to all the doctors and specialists we would care to see, and that we lived within just a short drive of Lombardi's world-class facilities. I particularly remember Robin's saying how grateful she was that we hadn't chosen to try saving money by enrolling with an HMO. We were lucky yuppies, and we knew it.

Yet the more time we spent in the Lombardi Center and Georgetown hospital, the more I was disturbed by the way they managed "the little things." On the day Robin underwent her lumpectomy, for example, I had to explain to her afterwards as best I could why I wasn't there to offer her support and comfort when she awoke. The reason, though hard for both of us to believe at the time, was that no one in the hospital could tell me, despite my increasingly frantic inquiries, where she was. I had imagined that every hospital, particularly a prestigious one attached to a major university in the nation's capital, operated with advanced information technology systems that kept track of every patient's location and condition. Not true, it turns out.

I was similarly shocked at how little the various specialists involved in her care seemed to consult with one another, or to keep up to date on the results of tests. In one emotionally devastating meeting, for example, the discussion began with various members of Robin's "team" optimistically discussing her prospects for reconstructive surgery. Robin and I were both thrilled that the lumpectomy was an apparent success and that her chemotherapy seemed to be working to contain the cancer. But well into the meeting, one doctor began to fidget, finally asking if anyone had looked at the results of a recent liver scan. The team quickly departed, leaving Robin and me in an empty examining room for 30 or 40 minutes. Eventually, a grim-faced oncologist returned. The cancer had metastasized to her liver. It looked as if she was terminal.

As I said, I never blamed her doctors for her death, but seeds of doubt sprouted in my mind about the system in which they were operating. Most of the doctors were sympathetic enough, and all were highly credentialed. But there seemed to be little attention given to managing information and coordinating care. It was as if, upon arriving at an airline gate, you were informed that the airline had lost track of the plane, couldn't find its passenger manifest, and couldn't say if it had passed its last inspection. At any given time, Robin's medical records and test results seemed to be scattered in paper files kept by different departments. If any one doctor played the role of pilot, much less air traffic controller, I had no idea who he or she was.

The experience of Robin's treatment set off unsettling questions in my mind, though I tried to suppress them. Who was in charge of quality control? Why did everything seem to be done on the fly? Why did almost every routine process—doctor visits, lab tests, chemotherapy sessions—seem to involve interminable waits or changes in plan? I couldn't offer Robin any comfort either when she received the news that she only had an estimated 17 days to live and would have to go home from the hospital to die. A doctor had changed his mind without telling us about when he would share with us the results of Robin's latest tests. And so she received this death sentence while alone in the hospital and had no one to talk to about it for hours. In a normal business, like, say, an airline, being perpetually late and having to shift plans constantly are sure signs that its processes are breaking down and that something bad is waiting to happen.

Then there were all the logistical and insurance issues. When was someone going to change her IV? When could our two-year-old son visit her? How long could she stay in the hospital after she had been declared terminal? How could one arrange for home hospice care, what did it cost, and who would pay? I came away feeling that no patient should ever enter a hospital without having some kind of full-time advocate—a caring, calm, and shrewd relative or friend at least, preferably with medical training and a law degree—to help navigate all the potential perils. And I wondered why the American health care system, or at least this one prestigious corner of it, had come to be like this.

A short time after Robin died, I read in the newspaper that the Institute of Medicine had issued a landmark report in which it estimated that up to 98,000 Americans are killed every year in hospitals as a result of medical errors—a toll which exceeds that of AIDS, breast cancer, or even motor vehicle accidents. The article also put it another way: It was like three jumbo jets crashing every other day and killing all on board. I was shocked, but upon reflection, not incredulous.[1]

Indentured Servitude

Another reason I was eager to accept *Fortune*'s assignment was that the American health care crisis seemed finally to be coming to a head. As long ago as 1970, the editors of *Fortune* had put out a special issue on medical care, declaring it "on the brink of chaos." *BusinessWeek*, that same year, had a cover story on American health care entitled "$60 Billion Crisis." But health care by now was close to a $2 *trillion* crisis, and that didn't even count all the indirect costs it was imposing on the economy and Americans' pursuit of happiness.

One of those indirect costs that I had experienced firsthand, along with millions of other Americans, was finding myself trapped in a job by my need for insurance. Shortly after Robin's cancer was diagnosed, *U.S. News* went through a management shakeup. The editor who had hired me was summarily fired, and I found myself on the losing side of a regime change. The jig was up, and it was time for me to go.

But, though I had several tempting offers, I had to stay and tough it out as best I could because I could not risk changing insurance plans with Robin's preexisting condition. As it turned out, I was fortunate to be able to keep my job for as long as I had to, and I'm very grateful to all involved for that. But the experience sensitized me to how many Americans are stuck in place year after year—unable to start a new business, go back to school, or even take time off to care for a loved one—just because of the way we finance our health care system.

I was also aware, of course, of the many familiar trend lines that make our health care system unsustainable. Two years before Robin died, when our son was born prematurely at just 2H pounds, I was amazed by and grateful to doctors and nurses at Sarasota Memorial Hospital who managed to keep him alive. But during the 60 days he was in the neonatal intensive care ward, I came to know other parents of "preemies" who, regardless of whether they lost their babies, were losing their homes and headed toward bankruptcy because they lacked health insurance. Since then, the number of such tragedies has only grown.

Every year, the cost of health care rises faster than the economy grows, with results that are as predictable as they are depressing. Because of its soaring price, we see millions of workers forced to forgo raises and to assume more and more of the cost of their health care, even if they are still lucky enough to have group insurance. We see the ranks of the uninsured swelling year after year, and the crush of medical expenses emerging as the number one source of personal bankruptcy.[2] We see once-proud corporations like General Motors made insolvent and forced to downsize or go out of business in large part because of their ruinous liabilities for employee and retiree health care benefits. We see state and local governments raising taxes and the federal government going deeper and deeper in debt as they try to cover the exploding cost of publicly financed health care programs.

And all this is before the baby boomers, my generation, begin experiencing the infirmities and chronic illnesses of old age. Projections for Medicare and Medicaid alone show that if the cost of these two programs continues growing even at a rate below their historical average, they will wind up consuming more than 20 percent of the nation's Gross Domestic Product (GDP) before the last of the boomers pass, or as big a share of the economy as is consumed by the entire federal government today.[3]

Health Care's Declining Pace of Progress

A final reason I was eager to take on *Fortune*'s assignment was a little-known but diabolical fact I had stumbled upon shortly after Robin died. The more I thought about it, the more alarming and outrageous it seemed to me. I discovered it after reading a study by the Federal Reserve that calculated how many hours, in different eras, the average American worker had to be on the job in order to make enough money to purchase various big-ticket items.

The study showcased the example of cars. Back in 1955, for instance, the average worker had to labor 1,638 hours to earn enough to buy a brand new Ford Fairlane. By 1997, the average American worker earned enough in just 1,365 hours to buy a brand new Ford Taurus, which, unlike the Fairlane, came with such standard features as air conditioning, airbags, cruise control, and power windows, steering, and brakes, and it got much better mileage. According to the study, a similar pattern of improving quality at lower real cost is true of nearly every big-ticket item for sale in the American economy.[1]

But what, I wondered, would happen if one included the cost of health care, which the study did not? It's a simple calculation, and when I did the math, the results were as devastating as they were revealing. If you've ever wondered how the nation's per capita GDP can grow year after year without most Americans feeling any richer, here's a big part of the explanation.

Let's travel back to 1964, for example. Most Americans are feeling prosperous. Suburbia is burgeoning. Record numbers of American youth are becoming the first in their families to go to college. Intellectuals complain about the miseries of "The

Affluent Society." Yet the average American worker takes home only $2.53 an hour. How does that square? You can't just say that a dollar went further in those days, because as we've just seen, the real cost of cars and just about every other consumer item has actually declined since that era. But there is a ready explanation. While workers in the 1960s had to put in many more hours on the job to purchase items like televisions, cars, or a ride in an airplane, they hardly had to work at all to cover the cost of health care.

At the time, health care spending in the United States was just $197 per person per year. This meant that with a mere 78 hours of labor (or by the end of the second work week in January for those working full time) the average worker earned enough to cover the per capita cost of health care, including that of all children and retirees. By contrast, in 2004, despite massive improvements in productivity outside the health care sector, the average worker had to put in *390* hours before earning enough to cover the average per capita burden of medical expenses, which by then had risen to over $6,200. Put another way, in that year it was well into March before average Americans, working a 40-hour week, earned enough to pay the health care sector's growing claim on their output.

Given current trends in wages and health care spending, by 2054, the average American worker will need to put in 2,970 hours a year to cover the cost of health care. That would mean working at least 8 hours a day, every day of the year, from January to December, with all of life's needs outside of health care somehow financed by still more exertion. So much for the Affluent Society. Obviously, something big is going to give.

It gets worse when you think about it. What kind of health care did Americans get back in 1964 for just $197? For those too young to remember that era, health care back then was far from primitive. A strong memory I have from childhood is that of my maternal grandfather explaining to me, sometime in the mid-'60s, how he could not in good conscience continue practicing medicine because it had become too sophisticated, complicated, and fast paced for him to follow any longer. He had graduated from the University of Michigan's medical school in 1927 as part of a new generation of doctors whose training was rigorous, competitive, and grounded in science, and he had gone on to enjoy a distinguished career in medicine. But by the mid-1960s he felt out of his depth.

The operations performed in that era included open-heart surgery, the implanting of pacemakers, and neurosurgery for the treatment of Parkinson's disease and other neurological disorders. Electrocardiograms were in common use, and doctors had long since learned how to use defibrillation to jump start stalled hearts. My own mother almost died of a misdiagnosed appendicitis in the 1960s, but once the right diagnosis was made she was easily saved by an appendectomy, which by then had become a routine operation.

Thanks to the increasing use of kidney dialysis machines, death rates from kidney disease were also plunging. Anesthesia no longer just meant knocking patients out with ether; it included local anesthesia, pain management, resuscitation, oxygen therapy, and the use of mechanical ventilators to avoid lung complications in patients recovering from major surgery. The polio vaccine was fully developed, and tuberculosis was nearly vanquished, as were such once devastating child killers as diphtheria and whooping cough. Wonder drugs like penicillin and other new antibiotics had caused the death rate from pneumonia and other infectious diseases to plummet.

In all the time I spent growing up in the 1960s, I knew only one classmate who died from a childhood disease, and knew none who lost a parent to illness. Then, as now, cancer patients were treated with prolonged chemotherapy, the development of which had been generously supported by government funding since the mid-1950s. Doctors did not yet have PET scans or MRIs, but X-rays achieved much the same purpose and in any event required expensive equipment and highly trained personnel.

The quality of doctors was also very high. Long gone were the quacks who had typified American medicine at the beginning of the century. By the 1960s, even elderly doctors, such as my maternal grandfather, had undergone medical training that was as prolonged and exacting as that received by doctors today, including a minimum of four years of medical school and at least a one-year, postgraduate internship. Though most physicians may not have lived up to the performance of such celebrated television doctors of the era as Marcus Welby, M.D., and Dr. Kildare, polling data clearly show that health care leaders in that era enjoyed a reputation for probity and professionalism that is long gone today.[5]

Hospitals in the 1960s also offered as high, and in some ways higher, levels of service than they typically do now. Private and semiprivate rooms were already the norm. In the 1960s, patients were also allowed to stay in the hospital much longer than today, which of course costs money. Not all of those extra days were medically necessary, but it would have been considered malpractice to send home patients who still required infusions or highly flammable oxygen tanks, as is routinely done today. Nor would hospitals simply send terminally ill patients home to die with a stash of morphine and some counseling from a social worker, which, as I discovered with Robin, is too often the present-day meaning of "hospice" care.

A Mexican acquaintance, who used to work in a store near our house, couldn't believe it when I told him, shortly after Robin died, the reason he hadn't seen me in 2 weeks. I explained that I'd been holed up with my mother at home, with barely time to eat or sleep, trying to tend to Robin in her final days while at the same time looking after a very upset and angry two-year-old who couldn't bear to watch his mother slowly die before his eyes. "In Mexico," the man said, shaking his head, "we never send people home to die."

Hospitals in the 1960s also routinely bore the cost of providing a calm, safe place for alcoholics to detox and for the emotionally distraught to have their "nervous breakdowns"— services that are today usually offered on an "outpatient" basis. Again, providing these services in the hospital was not always the most cost-effective option, but these services were part of what Americans got from the health care system for just $197 per year, or just 2 weeks' labor.

So why does the average American now have to work until mid-March of every year to earn the per capita cost of health care? Where is all this money going? and what improvements in health is it buying? Here the facts get even more outrageous. Yes, many individuals today owe their lives to treatments that were unavailable a generation ago. These notably include treatments in emergency rooms, which were still uncommon in the 1960s. We've also become much better at keeping underweight babies alive. Elective treatments like cataract surgery have improved the quality of many people's lives. And yes, since the passage of Medicare and Medicaid in 1965, the poor and elderly have far better access to health care than they previously did.

But for the population as a whole, the results in improved health and life expectancy are astonishingly modest. The rate of improvement in life expectancy, for example, actually slowed substantially after the explosion in health care spending that began in the 1960s. Between 1900 and 1960, life expectancy at birth in the United States increased by an average of 0.64 percent per year. From 1960 to 2002, however, that rate of improvement declined by 40 percent, to just 0.24 percent per year.[6] Moreover, the gains in life expectancy that have been achieved over the last forty years have come largely from broad social and technological trends as opposed to strictly medical interventions. For example, today's Americans smoke far less, drive far safer cars, run much less risk of being injured on the job, and are much less likely to be shot accidentally, to cite just four major nonmedical sources of increased longevity. From 1960 to 2002, the age-adjusted death rate from unintentional injuries, such as from car wrecks, firearm accidents, and on-the-job accidents, declined by 42 percent. Medicine can take credit for some of the increases to longevity over the last generation, but at least half of the improvement comes from nonmedical factors, such as mandatory airbags, gunlocks, and the great shift of the workforce away from farms, factories, and mines into less hazardous, service sector work. Epidemiologist John P. Bunker, a world-recognized authority on the determinants of health and longevity, estimates that only about 50 percent of the seven years of increased life expectancy at birth since 1950 is attributable to medical care.

This is true despite the astonishing increase in the cost and volume of medical care during that period.[7] According to Harvard health care economist David M. Cutler, in 1960, average Americans 65 and older consumed an inflation-adjusted $11,495 in health care during their remaining lifetime. By 2000, that number had jumped to $147,054. Yet despite this eleven-fold increase in health care spending per senior, the resulting gain in life expectancy was a mere 1.7 years.[8] Measured by its "rate of return," or the extra years of human life produced per health care dollar spent, American medicine is amazingly unproductive and inefficient.

Nor can we say that the increasing cost of health care just reflects the aging of the population. As the baby boomers slam into old age, population aging will indeed become a major source of increased demand for health care. But over the last 30 or forty years, the percentage of population over 65 has grown only modestly, and there is broad consensus among researchers that population aging has so far been a minor factor in driving health care costs. For example, the Center for the Study of Health System Change has found that from 1990 to 1995, spending increases due to population aging ranged from a mere 0.1 percent to 0.3 percent, primarily because baby boomers were then still relatively young.[9]

Instead, the big cause of skyrocketing health care costs has been increasingly intensive use of technologies and treatments that, when we look at their effects on the population as whole, have brought only negligible improvement in public health and longevity. Every year, for example, American cardiologists perform about 400,000 heart bypass surgeries and 1 million angioplasties—a procedure in which meshed tubes are placed in clogged arteries to hold them open. Yet recent studies show that only about 3 percent of the patients who receive such operations benefit from them; most would be better served just taking aspirin or low-cost beta blockers.[10]

Similarly, most back surgeries do not relieve pain, and many make it worse, as has been shown by numerous studies over the years. And of course, though treatment fads come and go, we're still waiting for any truly effective treatment for cancer, let alone a cure. I am grateful to this day that Robin and I instinctively resisted suggestions from her doctors that she opt for a bone marrow transplant combined with high-dose chemotherapy. In the 1990s, tens of thousands of breast cancer patients received this expensive, painful, and once faddish treatment before "modern" medicine eventually got around to doing clinical trials to see if it works. Turns out it doesn't.[11]

Americans spend more per person on health care than any other country, and have very little to show for it except more medical bills and lots of ineffective, unnecessary, and even harmful treatments. Americans, for example, pay twice as much per person as Britons for health care. Yet even though the British are more prone to drink heavily and are just as likely to smoke, they live longer and are far healthier.

This is true even among privileged members of both societies. For example, a study published in the *Journal of the American Medical Association* in 2006 found that the prevalence of diabetes among American college graduates aged 55 to 64 is 9.5 percent, as opposed to 6.1 percent among British college graduates of the same age. Even after one controls for the fact that Americans of all classes are more prone to obesity, the disparity remains, with Americans of all classes more likely than their counterparts in Great Britain to be suffering from diabetes, heart disease, and cancer.[12]

Even some Third World countries have equivalent life tables with the United States, despite minuscule spending on health care. In Costa Rica, for example, total health care expenditures per person come to just $383 a year.[13] And there are little more than half as many doctors per capita as in the United States.[14] Yet life expectancy at birth is seventy-seven years, exactly the same as in the United States. Moreover, though infant and child mortality rates are higher in Costa Rica than in the United States, the adult population has a substantially better chance of becoming elderly there than here. In the United States, the chances of dying between age 15 and 59 are 13.9 percent for men and 8.2 percent for women. In Costa Rica, the chances are 12.9 percent for men and 7.6 percent for women.[15]

American Health Care's Unexpected Champion

And so I was eager to accept *Fortune*'s assignment and set off to discover what had gone wrong with America's health care system and who could fix it. My assumptions going in were typical of those held by many Americans, particularly those with conservative, promarket views and instinctive distrust of government. For example, I assumed that the biggest single cause of the American health care crisis was that too many of us pay for most of our care using other people's money. Hadn't the big explosion in health care cost started after the enactment of Medicare and Medicaid, along with the vast expansion of tax-subsidized employer-provided health insurance plans?

Another underexamined assumption I brought to this project was that American health care, as inequitable and inefficient as it may be, was nonetheless the most scientifically advanced in the world. Didn't tens of thousands of rich foreigners fly in desperation to the United States every year in search of treatments they could not get at home? Outside of veterans hospitals and some chronically mismanaged and underfunded "St. Elsewheres," the American health care system seemed the envy of the world, even if it cost too much and left too many uninsured. And I believed this was true precisely because it was the least "socialized."

Yet, as I started asking experts for suggestions about who was delivering the highest-quality, most cost-effective, innovative, and scientifically driven health care in America, I kept hearing an answer I could not believe. It contradicted all that I thought I knew about health care and medical economics, indeed, about markets and governments in general. Yet these experts backed up their assertion by pointing me to study after study, all published in prestigious, peer-reviewed journals. These, too, I found literally incredible at first. If their claim was so true and obvious, why did so few Americans know about it? Why was there no talk of it in all our health care debates?

Yet the hardcore data were overwhelming. They were also confirmed by the testimony of ordinary patients and doctors I talked to, and eventually by the evidence before my own eyes when I started touring facilities. Moreover, when I reflected on all that Robin and I had experienced during our ordeal—the fragmented care and record keeping, the difficulty in keeping track of patients, the amount of effort devoted to gaming insurance paperwork, and above all our lack of a long-term relationship with the institutions that provided her care—it all started to make sense.

At first I was depressed by what I learned because it was so counterintuitive, so against the received wisdom of America's business class, that I knew the editors of *Fortune* would never feature it on their cover. And I was right. We agreed on a kill fee with no hard feelings. Business is business. But as I pondered the deeper implications of what I had learned, my depression lifted, and I became excited.

A solution to America's health care crisis does exist, I realized. Better than that, you don't have to rely on mere theoretical speculations or econometric simulations to see how it might work, nor do you have to wait around for a revolution in technology. You don't even have to travel to some far-off foreign country like Sweden, or even Canada, to see it in operation.

It's already up and running, right here in America, with hospitals and clinics located in every state, plus the District of Columbia and Puerto Rico. It is, in fact, the largest integrated health care system in the United States.

Most of its doctors have faculty appointments with academic hospitals. Over the years two have won the Nobel Prize for medicine. Its innovations have included the development of the CT scanner, the first artificial kidney, the development of the cardiac pacemaker, the first successful liver transplant, and the nicotine patch, plus many advanced prosthetic devices, including hydraulic knees and robotic arms.

Health care quality experts also hail it for its exceptional safety record, its use of evidence-based medicine, its health promotion and wellness programs, and its unparalleled adoption of electronic medical records and other information technologies. Finally, and most astoundingly, it's the only health care provider in the United States whose cost per patient has been holding steady in recent years, even as its quality performance is making it the benchmark of the entire health care sector.

Though comparatively few Americans, especially among coastal elites, have any contact with it these days, and even fewer qualify for its services, its example shows that it is possible to make vast improvements in the quality, safety, and effectiveness of the health care all Americans receive, and to do so for but a fraction of what an unreformed health care system would cost. We need only open our eyes, open our hearts, and open our minds.

ONE

Best Care Anywhere

Quick. When you read "veterans hospital," what comes to mind? Maybe you recall the headlines about the three decomposed bodies found near a veterans medical center in Salem, Virginia, in the early 1990s. Two turned out to be the remains of patients who had wandered off months before. The other patient had been resting in place for more than fifteen years. The Veterans Administration admitted that its search for the missing patients had been "cursory."[1]

Or maybe you recall images from movies like *Born on the 4th of July*, in which Tom Cruise plays an injured Vietnam vet who becomes radicalized by his shabby treatment in a crumbling, rat-infested veterans hospital in the Bronx. Sample dialogue: "This place is a fuckin' slum!"

By the mid-1990s, the reputation of veterans hospitals had sunk so low that conservatives routinely used their example as a kind of *reduction ad absurdum* critique of any move toward "socialized medicine." Here, for instance, is Jarret B. Wollstein, a right-wing activist and author, railing against the Clinton health care plan in 1994: "To see the future of health care in America for you and your children under Clinton's plan," Wollstein warned, "just visit any Veterans Administration hos-

1

pital. You'll find filthy conditions, shortages of everything, and treatment bordering on barbarism."[2]

Former congressman and one-time attorney for the Department of Veterans Affairs Robert E. Bauman made the same point in 1994, in a long and well-documented policy brief for the libertarian Cato Institute. "The history of the [VA] provides cautionary and distressing lessons about how government subsidizes, dictates, and rations health care when it controls a national medical monopoly."[3]

And so it goes today. If the debate is over health care reform, it won't be long before some free-market conservative will jump up and say that the sorry shape of the nation's veterans hospitals just proves what happens when government gets into the health care business. I made the same argument myself, in a book published in the mid-1990s.[4] Yet here's a curious fact that few conservatives or liberals know. Who do you think receives better health care? Medicare patients who are free to pick their own doctors and specialists? Or aging veterans stuck in those presumably filthy VA hospitals, with their antiquated equipment, uncaring administrators, and incompetent staff?

An answer came in 2003, when the prestigious *New England Journal of Medicine* published a study that used eleven measures of quality to compare veterans health facilities with fee-for-service Medicare. In all eleven measures, the quality of care in veterans facilities proved to be "significantly better."[5]

Here is another curious fact. The *Annals of Internal Medicine* in 2004 published a study that compared veterans health facilities with commercial managed care systems in their treatment of diabetes patients. In seven out of seven measures of quality, the VA provided better care.[6] A RAND Corporation study published in the same journal concluded that VA outperforms all other sectors of American health care in 294 measures of quality.[7]

Or consider this. In 2006, a study comparing the life expectancy of elderly patients in the care of the veterans health system with those enrolled in the Medicare Advantage Program showed that the mortality rates were "significantly higher" among the latter.[8]

It gets stranger. Pushed by large employers eager to know what they are buying when they purchase health care for their employees, the National Committee for Quality Assurance ranks health care plans on many different performance measures. These include how well they manage high blood pressure or adhere to such protocols of evidence-based medicine as prescribing beta-blockers for patients recovering from a heart attack. Winning NCQA's seal of approval is the gold standard in the health care industry. And who do you suppose is the highest ranking health care system? Johns Hopkins? Mayo Clinic? Massachusetts General? Nope. In every single category, the veterans health care system outperforms the highest-rated non-VA hospitals.[9]

Or consider what veterans themselves think. Sure, it's not hard to find vets who complain about difficulties in establishing eligibility. Many are rightly outraged that the Bush administration, presumably because of its ideological hostility to government-provided health care, has decided to deny previously promised health care benefits to veterans who don't have service-related illnesses or who can't meet a strict means test. Yet these grievances are about access to the system, not about the quality of care. Veterans groups tenaciously defend the VA health care system and applaud its turnaround. "The quality of care is outstanding," says Peter Gayton, deputy director for veterans affairs and rehabilitation at the American Legion. In 2006 the Legion listed among its top legislative priorities a bill that would entitle veterans to trade in their Medicare benefits for treatment by the VA.

For six consecutive years, the VA has received the highest consumer satisfaction ratings of any public or private sector health care system, according to surveys done by the National Quality Research Center at the University of Michigan. In the latest independent survey, 83 percent of VA hospital patients express satisfaction with the care they receive. This compares to 76 percent of Medicare and Medicaid patients.[10] One reason vets like the VA so much: they enjoy prompt efficient service, as a rule. A full 69 percent report being seen within twenty minutes of scheduled appointments (that's happened to me about once in my life), while 93 percent report being able to see a specialist within 30 days of the desired appointment.[11]

Outside experts agree that the VA has become an industry leader in safety and quality. Dr. Donald M. Berwick, president of the Institute for Healthcare Improvement and one of the nation's top health care quality experts, praises the VA's information technology and use of electronic medical records as "spectacular." The venerable Institute of Medicine notes that the VA's "integrated health information system, including its framework for using performance measures to improve quality, is considered one of the best in the nation."[12] The *Journal of the American Medical Association* noted in 2005 that the VA's health care system has "quickly emerged as a bright star in the constellation of safety practice."[13] Another study published in *JAMA* finds that the VA is also distinguished by its ability to overcome racial disparities in health care by doing a much better job than other health care providers in keeping African American patients alive.[14]

The Toyota of Health Care

Stranger still, all the while that VA has been winning these encomiums, it has tightly contained its cost per patient. Even as inflation in the rest of the health care sector has been running in double digits, the VA is not only raising the quality, safety, and effectiveness of the care it provides, it is also controlling costs. As Harvard's John F. Kennedy School of Government gushed, in awarding the VA a top prize in 2006 for innovation in government: "While the costs of healthcare continue to soar for most Americans, the VA is reducing costs, reducing errors, and becoming the model for what modern health care management and delivery should look like."[15]

Precise comparisons of year-to-year costs per patient are difficult, since the mix of patients changes over time as eligibility rules change, along with the amount of combat American forces face. But here's a suggestive statistic: Between 1995 and 2004, the cumulative increase in the VA's cost per enrollee was just 0.8 percent, while that of Medicare was a whopping 40.4 percent. Over the same period, the Medical Consumer Price Index increased by 39.4 percent.[16]

Or consider this measure of the VA's medical efficiency. Veterans enrolled in its health care system are as a group far older, sicker, poorer, and more prone to mental illness, homelessness, and substance abuse than the population as a whole. Half of all VA enrollees are over age sixty-five. More than a third smoke. One in five veterans has diabetes, compared with one in fourteen U.S. residents in general. Name any chronic disease—Alzheimer's, cancer, congestive heart failure, sclerosis of the liver—and a much higher percentage of veterans have it than do Americans in general. Yet the VA's average expenditure per patient in 2004 was just $5,562, including the prescription drug and long-term care benefits that have long been available to VA patients.[17] By comparison, Americans as a whole, including children and those who never saw a doctor during the year, consumed an average $6,280 in health care dollars in 2004.[18]

Admittedly, these comparisons are not perfect. Many people enrolled with the VA also receive health care elsewhere. Much of the VA's cost savings have resulted from closing obsolete or underutilized hospitals—a process that cannot continue indefinitely. And it is also true that the VA's cost per patient has risen somewhat in recent years. But remember, the population the VA serves is not only older, sicker, and poorer than the U.S. population as a whole, in recent years it has also been joined by all the soldiers wounded in Iraq and Afghanistan—many of whom, because of the use of body armor in these conflicts, are coming home with grievous injuries that otherwise would have killed them. The VA's ability to contain its cost per patient under these circumstances is truly remarkable.

You might well think that the untold story here is that the VA engages in rationing. And indeed, according to a RAND study published in the *New England Journal of Medicine* in 2006, VA patients received only about 67 percent of the care that experts believe they should get. But before you say, "I knew there was a catch," consider this: the same study found that the U.S. health care system as a whole delivers only 54.9 percent of the treatments recommended by evidence-based medicine.[19]

Because the VA lacks any financial incentive to engage in overtreatment, it saves money by avoiding unnecessary surgery and redundant testing. But "rationing" is hardly the right word to explain the VA's cost-effectiveness. Instead, it is Americans who *don't* use the VA who stand the greatest risk of receiving inappropriate care, ranging from doctors who fail to prescribe routine preventive measures such as flu vaccines or medicine to control hypertension to vast amounts of overtreatment. According to the same study, even Americans with $50,000 or more in family income receive lower-quality health care than do VA patients in general.[20]

What a concept! Cost containment and quality improvement go hand in hand in many industries, but in health care this is virtually unheard of. If the VA were a car company, it would be Toyota. Today's VA produces the equivalent of well-engineered, efficient, reliable, reasonably priced cars with few defects and great safety records, using proven scientific techniques and a culture of continuously improving quality control. By contrast, if America's most prestigious hospitals were auto companies, most would build cars like Alfa Romeo or Renault—classy to look at, and often very innovative, but unsafe, inefficient, temperamental, ridiculously expensive, and an unwise choice of transportation in situations where your life actually depends on their not breaking down.

Take-Home Lessons

If this contrast gives you cognitive dissonance, it should. The VA, after all, is a massive bureaucracy headquartered in Washington. Its medical division alone, known as the Veterans Health Administration (VHA), employs more than 198,000 workers represented by five different unions. Even many of its doctors are organized into bargaining units. This is the last place most people, including myself, would expect to find true innovation in technology or human organization, let alone a world-class exemplar of best practices in health care.

The VA's performance is particularly difficult for conservatives to process. Back in 2004, when the Bush administration pushed for greater use of information technology in health care as a means of improving quality and holding down costs, it wound up choosing not some well-endowed, prestigious private hospital as the place to showcase the potential, but the Baltimore VA Medical Center. That's because, despite the administration's overall faith in market forces, it could find no private sector hospital that could begin to match the VA's use of electronic medical records. Only about 10 percent of American hospitals even have them, and those that do often find their commercial software programs to be buggy and inadequate. "I know the veterans who are here are going to be proud to hear that the Veterans Administration is on the leading edge of change," Bush found himself exclaiming in his remarks at the Baltimore VA Medical Center.[21] If Bush found it strange or disorienting to be saying this about the largest actual example of socialized medicine in the United States, he didn't express any curiosity about how and why it might be true.

Which is regrettable. Because the story of how and why the VA became the benchmark for quality medicine in the United States suggests that vast swaths of what we think we know about health, health care, and medical economics are just wrong.

It's natural to believe, for example, as I long did, that more competition and consumer choice in health care will lead to greater quality and lower costs, because in almost every other realm it does. That's why the Bush administration and conservatives in general have pushed for individual "health savings accounts" and high-deductible insurance plans. Together, these measures are supposed to encourage patients to do more comparison shopping and haggling with their doctors, and therefore create more market discipline in the system.

But when it comes to health care, it's a government bureaucracy that's setting the standard for best practices while controlling costs, and it's the private sector that's lagging in quality and cost-effectiveness. That unexpected reality needs examining if we're to have any hope of understanding what's wrong with America's health care system and how to fix it.

It turns out that precisely because the VA is a big, government-run system that has nearly a lifetime relationship with its patients, it has incentives for investing in prevention and effective treatment that are lacking in private-sector medicine. As we'll see, these incentives became particularly sharp beginning at the VA's lowest moment in the late 1970s. Even as the VA faced severe budget cuts and loss of political support, the large numbers of World War II and Korean War veterans it served were then beginning to experience the infirmities of old age. VA doctors in that era found themselves dealing more and more with aging patients beset by chronic conditions such as hypertension, diabetes, and cancer, and they had to find a way to manage these diseases with dwindling resources. The happy, if unexpected, result was an explosion of organizational and technological innovation, most of it started by individual VA doctors acting on their own, that the private sector still cannot match.

During the period of the VA's transformation, chronic illnesses still affected a comparatively small share of the population as a whole but are now becoming widespread as the baby boom generation ages and as increasing numbers of younger Americans experience the consequences of obesity and sedentary lifestyle. This gives the story of the VA's turnaround a growing relevancy. Some twenty years ahead of their time, VA doctors felt compelled to begin developing a new, highly effective model of care stressing prevention as well as safe and effective management of chronic disease. Today, the continuing improvement of this model, which is based largely on the skillful use of information technology in both treatment and medical research, has propelled the VA into the vanguard of twenty-first century medicine. The purpose of this book is to explain the VA's unexpected triumph and to show how to make its benefits available to all Americans.

TWO

Hitting Bottom

No other health care provider in the United States has had such a scandal-filled and controversial past as the VA, and so it is no wonder that many Americans have long pointed to its example as proof that government-provided health care is a very bad idea. Yet a closer look at the checkered history of the VA reveals subtler lessons, both about how government-run institutions can and do fail and about how ordinary men and women can reinvent them—even over the objection of their bosses.

It is a story that begins with one of the biggest political scandals in American history. One afternoon in 1925, a visitor to the White House was mistakenly sent to "The Red Room" on the second floor. Approaching the door, the visitor encountered the commander in chief with his hands around a man's neck shouting "You yellow rat! You double-crossing bastard. If you ever . . ."[1]

The object of Warren G. Harding's wrath, so goes the story, was Colonel Charles R. Forbes. Forbes was a dashing and charismatic man, fond of playing poker and living the high life. Both Harding, and especially his wife, it was said, found him to be great company when they first met him while on vacation to Hawaii. "Colonel Forbes was the type of man around whom women always have buzzed," explained one Harding loyalist in his memoirs.[2]

But Forbes was also the type of man who, despite being a deserter in World War I, somehow became a colonel, winning the Congressional Medal, and enjoying a strong leadership role in the American Legion. And he was also the type of man who could win enough confidence from the president of the United States to be appointed to the politically sensitive and morally crucial role of heading up the newly formed Veterans Bureau, where he was tasked with organizing the health care of millions of wounded veterans of the Great War.

He was a poor choice, for he also turned out to be one of the greatest crooks ever to hold high office in the United States. By the time all the investigations were over, and Forbes had been sent off to serve hard time at Leavenworth, the total tally for his graft and flagrant waste of taxpayer dollars stood at $200 million, or about $2.1 billion in today's money. Forbes took lavish kickbacks on the various veterans hospitals he built around the country. For example, he used taxpayer dollars to pay more than five times the market value for the land on which the VA hospital in Livermore, California, still stands. For his troubles, he and a fellow partner in crime each pocketed $12,500 in kickbacks. When he wasn't touring the nation picking out other lucrative sites on which to build hospitals, he was entertaining extravagantly and living a life of luxury in Washington, ostensibly on his government salary of $10,000 a year.

To maintain his lifestyle, Forbes plied the Veterans Bureau with trainloads of unneeded provisions, such as a 100-year supply of floor wax, which he then sold off by the trainload for pennies on the dollar in exchange for kickbacks. Boxcars filled with bed sheets, drugs, alcohol, and other hospital supplies—

many desperately needed by overcrowded veterans hospitals—
would arrive at the railroad siding outside the Veterans
Bureau's warehouse in Perryville, Maryland, only to be re-
loaded out the back door almost immediately for resale as
"government surplus."

Not only was Forbes's graft extraordinary but he let down
millions of Great War veterans, many of them poisoned by
mustard gas and otherwise grievously wounded, thereby
making a "lost generation" feel even more abandoned. Reflect-
ing on his experience with Forbes and his cronies, Harding
would later famously say, "I have no trouble with my enemies.
I can take care of them. It is my friends. My friends that are
giving me trouble."[3]

Routineers and Mediocrities

Yet it wasn't just scandal, but attempts to avoid scandal, that
marred the veterans health system for much of its history.
One of the reasons the VA would later emerge as such a rule-
bound and ossified bureaucracy was that, after the example
of Charles Forbes, subsequent administrators were terrified
by the prospect of unauthorized spending and insider graft.
The first of these was Brig. Gen. Frank T. Hines. One chroni-
cler of the VA describes him as a "bald-pated, slightly built
shipbuilding businessman who spent the next twenty-two
years trying to keep the Veterans Bureau (and beginning in
1930, the Veterans Administration) from the pit of financial
corruption."[4]

In 1945, muckraking journalist Albert Deutsch testified before Congress about the type of bureaucracy Hines had
created:

He placed excessive stress on paper work. Bureaucratic procedures were developed, which tied up the organization in needless red tape. Avoidance of scandal became the main guide of official action. Anything new was discouraged: "It might get us in trouble." Routineers and mediocrities rose to high office by simple process of not disturbing the status quo. Good men were frozen out or quit . . . the agency increasingly was controlled by old men with old ideas.[5]

After World War II, Omar Bradley, the storied "soldier's general," took over the Veterans Administration for two years and did much to bring its health services into the modern age. At the time, the nation's newspapers were full of headlines like, "Veterans Hospitals Called Backwaters of Medicine" and "Third-Rate Medicine for First-Rate Men." In an attempt to turn the situation around and prepare for the huge wave of returning World War II veterans, Bradley had a memorandum sent to the deans of the nation's medical schools offering them an attractive deal. They could partner with local veterans hospitals and use their facilities to help train medical internists and residents, while also having their faculties control hiring and firing decisions.[6]

This was a fateful decision that changed the course of the VA, and of American health care as a whole. Today, an estimated 65 percent of all doctors practicing in the United States have received all or part of their training in VA facilities. The deep collaboration with the nation's medical schools also helped the VA to raise the caliber of its doctors and led to veterans hospitals enjoying much better reputations, at least among the World War II generation of veterans.

One prime example is former senator Bob Dole, who remains grateful for the prolonged treatment he received in veterans hospitals after being strafed by Nazi machine gun fire during the final weeks of World War II. He married his nurse and spoke movingly throughout his life about the men and women who helped him for over two years to recover from his paralysis. The VA, which also did a capable job of administering the generous educational and housing benefits extended to World War II vets under the GI bill, enjoyed a golden moment of high public esteem.

But the moment was fleeting. By the mid-1950s, Congress was already rapidly cutting the VA's budget, causing massive layoffs. Many Korean War vets discovered they could not get into VA hospitals unless they could prove they had service-related disabilities. At the same time, a census taken in 1954 found that 65 percent of patients had been in VA hospitals for more than 90 days and that 8 percent had been in the hospital for over twenty years! Many VA hospitals remained little better than warehouses for the homeless, the infirm, and the aged.[7]

It was also true, however, that, thanks to its affiliation with medical schools, the VA continued to distinguish itself by developing many innovative medical techniques. During the 1950s, Rosalyn Yalow did her work in nuclear medicine at a VA hospital in the Bronx that would later earn her the Nobel Prize. In the early 1960s, endocrine oncologist Andrew V. Shalley was doing the experiments in his lab at the New Orleans VA hospital that would make him a Nobel laureate as well. In the early 1970s, the VA became the first health care provider in the United States to install nuclear-powered heart pacemakers.

But there were also recurring instances of veterans being subjected to medical experiments and treated as guinea pigs.

As early as 1950, fourteen VA hospitals, all affiliated with medical schools, were performing radiation experiments on patients under the VA's radioisotope program. Yet, while these experiments may have advanced the cause of science, there is no record that the VA even contemplated a program for acquiring informed consent until 1958.[8]

Ironically, in the course of testing the effects of LSD in the early 1960s the VA hospital in Palo Alto, California, gave it to a man named Vic Lovell, who enjoyed "the trip" so much that he "turned on" his friend and neighbor Ken Kesey to the psychedelic experience. Kesey got himself a job at the VA to secure his supply, eventually stealing LSD from the hospital when the trials were over. While tripping with schizophrenics in the hospital's psychiatric ward, Kesey received the inspiration, he would later say, for his masterpiece, *One Flew Over the Cuckoo's Nest*. He and his band of Merry Pranksters went on to make "acid" seem cool to a whole generation of Americans.[9]

Broken Promises

At around the same time, veterans started returning from Vietnam to an ungrateful nation. Maybe it was the lucky ones who were treated to mind-altering drugs. Not only did many returning Vietnam vets find veterans hospitals woefully underfunded and run down, many found them staffed by people they regarded as hostile. Some were house officers and doctors their own age who opposed the war and had avoided the draft by going to medical school. Others were older vets who viewed Vietnam veterans as losers and who dismissed their complaints about posttraumatic stress and exposure to chemical agents like Agent Orange as unmanly. It wasn't until 1978 that the VA even set up a registry of veterans exposed to the 19 million gallons of Agent Orange and other dioxin-laden defoliants dropped on Vietnam. It wasn't until the 1990s that the VA stopped demanding that Vietnam veterans exposed to Agent Orange offer proof. And only then did the VA begin to presume, for purposes of establishing eligibility for treatment, that conditions such as diabetes and some cancer may well have been caused by such exposure.

Many Vietnam veterans were also insulted by the conditions they found in veterans hospitals. In an autobiography that later became the movie *Born on the 4th of July*, Ron Kovic, a two-tour marine who was severely injured in Vietnam, told the story of his experience in a veterans hospital in the Bronx. After describing how the hospital lacked the equipment he needed as an amputee to learn how to walk again, he quoted a young doctor's matter-of-fact explanation that it is all because of the war. "The government is not giving us money for the things we need."

The result of all these tensions, hard feelings, and strained budgets was something approaching complete institutional failure at many veterans hospitals. Part of the problem was that, thanks to improvements in combat medicine and air evacuation, many Vietnam veterans were men who would have died of their wounds in previous wars, and who were now coming home instead with severe injuries and disabilities. But that was hardly an excuse for the conditions many of them faced. Activists among the new generation of vets did everything they could to draw media and public attention to the failings of various veterans hospitals, even if it sometimes meant exaggerating how bad they were.

One of those activists was Oliver Meadows, a former commander of Disabled American Veterans and staff director of the House Veterans Affairs Committee. He would later proudly recall how he and others "literally staged specials with ABC, NBC, CBS. We staged the network spectaculars. We had major articles in *Reader's Digest*, *Life* magazine. They were all over the country. We had a specially tailored story written for St. Louis, for example, and the local papers would pick it up. Every VA hospital in the country was covered. We released material to those papers where the hospital was located."[10]

On May 22, 1970, *Life* published a photo essay about conditions in the Kingsbridge VA hospital in the Bronx that fixed the reputation of veterans hospitals in the post-Vietnam era. The story quoted a quadriplegic lance corporal: "Nobody should have to live in these conditions. We're all hooked up to urine bags, and without enough attendants to empty them, they spill over the floor. It smells and cakes something awful. . . . It's like you've been put in jail, or you've been punished for something." Worst of all, the lance corporal continued, were the rats.

Meadows would later say the *Life* story "was totally contrived, we helped them all the way." And indeed, according to Robert Klein, author of the 1981 book, *Wounded Men, Broken Promises*, which is generally an exposé of veterans hospitals, some VA officials, and at least one veteran interviewed for the *Life* story, claimed that conditions in the various VA hospitals were actually staged by activists to make them look more awful and sensational than they really were. Yet there is also no doubt that many veterans hospitals in this era had sunk into squalor and become little better than medical slums.

During the Carter years, the VA was headed by Max Cleland, himself a Vietnam veteran and a triple amputee, who would later use his considerable political skills to become a U.S. senator from Georgia and a Democratic Party icon. Yet during his tenure at the VA, many vets came to believe that Cleland had been "fragged" by his own men in Vietnam and resented his attempts to portray himself as one of them. Furious at Cleland's refusal to acknowledge the link between exposure to Agent Orange and their subsequent cancers and disabilities, a throng of Vietnam vets came close to physically attacking Cleland in his wheel chair during a Senate hearing, taunting "Did you lose your balls in Vietnam, too?"

The Iron Triangle

Probably the only reason the veterans health system survived this era was the "iron triangle" of inside politics. Medical schools benefited from their access to, and in many cases, control over, veterans hospitals. The major veterans service organizations, whose leadership often wound up being appointed to high positions in the VA, wanted the system improved and expanded, not eliminated, as did the public employee unions that represented much of the VA workforce. Politicians benefited from the jobs and money the VA brought to their communities, to say nothing of "free" health care the VA provided to indigent and low-income vets who otherwise would have become a local responsibility.

Even those politicians who believed that "patriotism should be its own reward," and who regarded the veterans hospitals as "socialized medicine" gone predictably amok, did not feel comfortable voting to close veterans hospitals, and found it easy not to. To this day, the various conservative organizations that rank members of Congress do not count votes for veterans benefits as examples of supporting the welfare state, but as votes for national defense.

And so the checkered course of the VA continued. Fortunately, however, in the deepest recesses of the VA's moribund bureaucracy, a quiet revolution, initially driven by a few lowly dissidents—some idealistic computer geeks, others idealistic doctors, pharmacists, and other medical personnel—had been set in motion. It was a revolution from below that, once embraced by charismatic new leadership, would lead to the VA's becoming by the end of the century a world leader in safe, high-quality, and innovative health care. The revolution got ugly at times. At one point, a suspicious fire damaged one of the dissident's computers. Others were forced to quit or were driven into effective exile. "There were some nasty, nasty games played," recalls one participant. But in the end, not even the most entrenched plutocrats in the VA's Washington office, nor their enablers in political office, could put down the insurrection of the so-called Hard Hats, as the dissidents came to call themselves.

THREE

Revenge of the Hard Hats

Dr. Kenneth Dickie still shudders at the memory. One day in 1979, someone snuck into his secret office in the basement of the VA Washington Medical Center. The intruder stacked piles of patient records around Dickie's DEC minicomputer, doused them with a flammable material, and set them on fire. Smoke filled the room, but, fortunately for Dr. Dickie and for the future of American health care, an alarm went off in time, and the computer he was using to build the country's first practical electronic medical record system was spared. Still, Dr. Dickie recounts today, he had to have the engine of his car rebuilt several times during this period because someone kept putting salt or sand into the gas tank.

Dickie was one of the Hard Hats who developed what is today known as the VA's VistA software program. VistA is actually a bundle of nearly 20,000 software programs, most of which were originally written in the 1970s and 1980s by individual doctors and other professionals working secretly in VA facilities around the country. These pioneers had to do their best to hide their work from their superiors because it violated VA policy and was threatening enough to elements within the VA to provoke literal sabotage. But eventually, working without a plan and without a leader, these dissident doctors would wind up creating a wonder of "bottom-up" engineering that many experts say points the way to the future of twenty-first century health care.

Today, after a long bureaucratic war that still leaves some of its developers congregating in online support groups, VistA has radically transformed the practice of medicine within the VA and made possible a new model of health care that is now being emulated around the world. This unique, integrated information system has dramatically reduced medical errors at the VA while also vastly improving diagnoses, quality of care, scientific understanding of the human body, and the development of medical protocols based on hard data about what drugs and procedures work best.

The story of how VistA first came to be is inspirational on many levels. For one, it is a shining example of a time when the "Dilberts" of the world won and their hidebound bosses were humiliated. Indeed, one of the ironies is that if the VA's leadership hadn't been so moribund for so long, the revolution that led to VistA would probably never have happened. A more "with it" leadership at the VA probably would have contracted out with some private software developer to provide its information systems. The most likely result would have been computer programs imposed on, instead of created by, doctors and other medical professionals, costing billions of dollars and written in a buggy proprietary code that ordinary users would have no ability to improve, modify, or integrate.

This is a familiar story in the world of American health care, where what few electronic medical information systems are in place often inspire resistance and fail. That's what happened for example, at Cedars-Sinai Medical Center in Los Angeles, which in 2003 turned off its brand-new, computerized physician order entry system. Doctors complained that it took five minutes or more to log into the system and to enter the patient and medication data needed to fill a prescription. At least six other hospitals have shut down computerized drug dispensing systems in recent years.[1]

But precisely because of its ossified traditions, the VA avoided this path. When its management failed to deliver workable information technology, the happy, if unintended, result was that various VA employees took it upon themselves to solve their own individual programming needs. Their individual efforts eventually created a highly effective hospital information system that remains unrivaled by any health care software developed by the private sector.

In 2003, the Bush administration's top man at the Centers of Medicare and Medicaid Services, Thomas Scully, chastised private software developers for failing to come up with programs that could even begin to match the performance of VistA—let alone its price. VistA is "open-source" software, meaning that the code itself is free to anyone who cares to download it off the Internet, and is accessible to individuals who care to modify it for their own purposes or to improve its performance. (Check out the demo at http://www1.va.gov/CPRSdemo.) The only function VistA can't do as well as its private-sector counterparts, at least without adding some code, is tracking patient billing. Instead, because of its origins, its focus is on patient care—something the private sector just can't seem to imitate.

Cubicle Wars

VistA's origins lie in the late 1970s. Like most large institutions of the era, the VA had committed to large, centralized, mainframe computers, such as the IBM 650 Magnetic Drum Data Processing Machine, which it had been using since the 1950s for administrative purposes. These machines were jealously guarded by a tight circle of "high priests," working out of the VA's central offices and its main computer center in Hines, Illinois, who regarded anything involving bits and bytes as their exclusive preserve.

Predictably, as with many other institutions of the time, the software these high priests wrote, or more often procured from private vendors, wasn't very good, in large part because the people who actually had to use it had little role in its development. Among the many scandals that dogged the VA in the 1970s was the poor performance of its information systems, which at one point in early 1976 completely broke down, causing 647,000 checks to veterans to go unwritten or to arrive late.[2]

Nor were the high priests, whose fiefdom was known as the Office of Data Management and Telecommunications (ODM&T), much better at developing software with medical applications. One project ODM&T embarked on, which was supposed to provide doctors with a computer system they could use in laboratories, began in 1968 and wasn't ready for deployment until 1982. Just completing the VA's seventeen-step bureaucratic process for approving new software typically took a minimum of three years of paper shuffling on top of whatever time the actual writing of the program required. In 1980, the high priests estimated it would take them at least ten years to develop even a rudimentary patient treatment file that could be stored in the VA's mainframes.[3]

But as it happened, this was the dawn of the era of mini- and personal computers, and a handful of technically minded doctors sprinkled throughout the VA began experimenting with writing their own software to meet their various needs. One was Kenneth Dickie, an internist at the VA Medical Center in Washington, D.C., who, in an attempt to simplify and improve his own working conditions, began working on a DEC minicomputer in the hospital's basement to develop a program that would combine lab results, patient history, and other data into a single electronic medical record. "It was unbelievably difficult to track down paper records," he recalls today, "and unbelievably difficult to track down the data I wanted in those records." In this era before laptops and wireless modems, Dr. Dickie's idea was that doctors and nurses could use a single minicomputer on each ward to update, retrieve, and print out complete patient records.[4]

Meanwhile, Gordon Moreshead and Wally Fort in Salt Lake City began developing a clinical psychology data system to use in their own facility. Bob Lushene in St. Petersburg, Florida, developed online psychodiagnostic tests; Richard Davis in Lexington, Kentucky, was writing a nutrient analysis program for the treatment of diabetics; and Joe Tatarczuk in Albany, New York, was working to computerize nuclear medicine.[5]

Two other key players were Joseph (Ted) O'Neill and Martin E. Johnson. Both had been part of early government efforts to explore the potential of information technology in the practice of medicine. In late 1977, they found a new and precarious perch within the VA's Department of Medicine and Surgery (forerunner of today's VHA) and began working out of a small office, cryptically labeled "Computer Assisted System Staff," from which they conspired to build a network of programmers within the VA that came to be known as the Hard Hats. In December 1978 in Oklahoma City, O'Neill and Johnson managed to pull off a meeting of freelancing programmers within the VA and persuaded them to write in a common, user-friendly, open-source language and to share their code. But everyone had to be careful to work under the radar of those who controlled the VA's centralized mainframes, even if it meant writing code under difficult conditions.

For example, many of the freelance programmers were forced to work on "word processors" that lacked tape drives. This was because buying a true personal computer, let alone one of the era's minicomputers, would have, as one participant relates, "set off alarm bells in the Central Office back in Washington." Programming on a Wang designed for secretaries made sharing information and updating software very difficult. The only way to do it was either with error-prone 300-baud modems or by physically carrying disk packs the size of cake trays from one site to another—a process some characterized as "committing portability."[6] Another key programmer, named George Timson, worked out of San Francisco by remote access ("quite unauthorized and quite unpaid-for," he states) with a Massachusetts firm to develop an elegant and highly effective file-sharing protocol that would become the heart of VistA.[7]

Yet, soon enough, the Hard Hats ran into trouble from the high priests who manned the VA mainframes. Many Hard Hats were fired or demoted; others had their computers confiscated. According to Timson,

> in one case, in Columbia, Bob Wickizer went to lunch, and found, when he got back to his computer room, that his new PDP-11/70 [a mini-computer made by Digital] had been unplugged and was in the process of being crated. By all ac-

counts, the machine never again processed another instruction, anywhere. "The Enemy" had won—or so it seemed.[8]

Yet this was not enough to appease the high priests. ODM&T ordered not only that Hard Hats stop writing new software but that their programs already in use be ripped out, including one that had automated admission and discharge processes, another used in radiology, and a third used in pharmacies. In 1979, ODM&T bureaucrats actually removed more hospital computer systems than they installed, all in an attempt to squash the innovation.[9] Part of their argument at the time was that this "helter-skelter" field development would get the VA in trouble with watchdog agencies like the Office of Management and Budget; indeed, investigations were launched about all the small computers and word processors the Hard Hats were ordering.[10] But Hard Hat Thomas Munnecke had another take. "I call this the 'hungry dinosaur syndrome,'" he later explained. "A centralized computing department gets so big and inflexible that it cannot adapt to changing technology."[11]

Despite the harassment they faced, the Hard Hats pressed forward in their clandestine efforts, and they were increasingly encouraged by doctors and other colleagues who found their software useful and effective. The Hard Hats had one crucial advantage: they were creating software either for their own use or for their colleagues. "I spent the whole weekend in Minneapolis sitting right next to a pharmacist," Greg Kreis remembers. "I would program it and try various things, and I would say, 'How does it look?' and he would say, 'Okay, let me check it.' He would check it and try and he would give me some ideas, and we coded furiously all weekend long to try to get some ideas working and make it speed up."[12]

The "Underground Railroad"

The turning point finally came in late 1981. By then, on orders from the central office, personal and minicomputers had been ripped out and locked up in closets where doctors couldn't get to them. The VA's central office had ordered a radiology system developed by Hard Hats in Columbia, Missouri, to be shut down. It had also pulled the plug on a pharmacy system under development in Birmingham, Alabama, and another one in Albany, New York.[13] When word leaked out to academic researchers of a promising patient discharge program developed by VA employees in Oklahoma City, the central office refused even to acknowledge its existence in public.

Stunned by these developments, many doctors and other medical professionals who used Hard Hat software and saw its value at last broke out in open rebellion. The controversy, which burst into the medical trade press and caught the attention of Congress, finally caused the VA's Chief Medical Director, Dr. Donald L. Custis, to take a field trip to the VA's Washington Medical Center on North Capitol Street to see what all the fuss was about.

This facility is only six miles away from the Central Office on Vermont Avenue near the White House, but in those days it was also a world away. This is where Kenneth Dickie, joined by Marty Johnson, labored secretly in the basement, developing electronic medical record software. It was also where another key ally of the Hard Hats, the late Paul Shafer, practiced surgery while also serving as executive director of the National Association of VA Physicians. When Custis arrived at the hospital, its director, A.A. Gavazzi, told him straight off that the Hard Hats enjoyed "100 percent" support from the hospital's doctors.

Custis observed all the homemade software systems in use, and also all the programs clandestinely imported from other Hard Hat strongholds around the country. These included programs that recorded drug prescriptions, printed pharmacy labels, analyzed psychological tests, maintained tumor registries, and much more. All were running on a DEC PDP 1134 minicomputer that Custis's office had expressly forbidden to be used for such purposes. But despite the obvious insubordination, Custis came away impressed. "It sounds like an 'underground railway' has been at work," he was heard to say, "and doing good work."[14]

Some Hard Hats started calling themselves members of the "underground railroad" and even had business cards printed up with a drawing of a steam engine. But soon, this railroad was underground no longer. Swayed by Custis's report of what he'd seen, and fed up with the recurring problems with the VA's formal computer division, the new Reagan administration's top appointees to the VA, Robert P. Nimmo and his deputy, Chuck Hagel (the future U.S. senator from Nebraska), signed off on the Hard Hats' initiatives and pulled the plug on the high priests.

Key allies in Congress, such as Rep. G.V. (Sonny) Montgomery, concurred. A conference report that would later take on historical irony noted that "Any further delay in proceeding with the decentralized . . . system is not justified and will only result in VA's medical computer system falling further behind the private health care industry."[15] Hundreds of high priests got riffed—government parlance for laid off. And within a short while, recalls Hard Hat Richard Davis, "Many highly labor intensive and error prone systems of daily operations within the VA medical centers were dismantled." The Hard Hats had won.

Fortunately, all the different programs that became VistA were written in an easy to use, common language, called MUMPS, that lent itself to integration and file sharing. This meant that they could all be fit together, in literally less than a week, into a central module. Eventually that module grew to include more programs, so that, for example, all the different forms of care a patient received, in all different parts of a hospital, as well as in clinics, could be combined into a single electronic health record.[16]

Catching the Age Wave Early

This might not at first seem like such a big deal. Even today, the potential of electronic health records to improve the practice of medicine is only beginning to become apparent to the public, or even to many private-sector health care providers. But individual doctors practicing within the VA were already in many ways living in the world of the future. As early as the 1970s, the population they served, which was dominated by veterans of World War II, was aging rapidly, much as the U.S. population as a whole is now beginning to experience a rapid increase in the number of elders.

This meant that VA doctors in the 1970s, like doctors everywhere today, were seeing increasing numbers of patients beset with complicated, chronic conditions like diabetes. These conditions, which were often accompanied by numerous co-morbidities such as high blood pressure and cardiovascular disease, required constant monitoring and coordinated care involving dozens of people—specialists, nurses, radiologists, lab workers, physical therapists, counselors. The nature of these chronic diseases also demanded that patients become vitally involved in their own care, such as in measuring their own blood sugar levels, and that a system be in place for keeping track of such measurements.

The comparative frailty of the population served by the VA also made patients exceptionally vulnerable to medical errors, such as different doctors prescribing dangerous combinations of drugs. The advancing age of the veterans population also put a premium on record keeping that could quickly pinpoint who, for example, was due for a flu shot or a prescription refill. Since patients approaching the end of life often consume high volumes of expensive treatment, VA doctors and administrators also had an exceptional need for data about which of these treatments worked better than others, and indeed, about which didn't work at all.

For all these reasons and more, the environment in which VA doctors were practicing medicine in the 1970s and '80s made the value of electronic health records and other information technology easier to see than in many private health care settings. Tellingly, Kenneth Dickie found his inspiration for developing electronic medical records while trying to contend with his caseload of VA nursing home patients in the 1970s.

A final and all-important consideration was that the VA as an institution maintained a near lifetime relationship with its patients. This meant there was a pressing institutional need to coordinate record keeping among the many different VA hospitals and clinics a veteran might use over his or her lifetime. And, crucially, it meant that any improvement to the quality of care the VA could achieve through its investment in information systems would rebound to its own long-term advantage. Managing diabetic care properly, for example, meant fewer expenditures for costly amputations down the road and would even help save on nursing home costs, for which the VA was potentially liable.

By contrast, in private-sector health care settings, where patients typically move on to another plan every few years, investment in preventing long-term complications more often than not brings no return to the institution. Thus, from a very early date, both VA doctors and administrators were far more likely than their private-sector counterparts to see the value of investing information technology that could improve the practice of medicine.

As Timson recalls,

> by the mid-80s everybody wanted everything. We finally kind of broke out of our illegitimate status as garage operations in different parts of the country and proved that we could put the pieces together. And then by the middle of the 80s we were building complete hospital information systems, using, of course, hardware that was laughably limited compared to the PC that's on your desk today.[17]

Private-sector vendors repeatedly pressured Congress to make VA doctors and technicians stop writing software. But VA doctors argued persuasively that there was no product available on the market that could compete with their own, user-made system.[18]

Since then, the growth in computer power and the emergence of the Internet, far from making VistA obsolete, has allowed it to grow still more capabilities. The original software is still in place in most facilities, but it is continually updated electronically with patches that fix bugs or add new features. Today these include electronic medical records containing X-rays, pathology slides, video views, scanned documents, cardiology exam results, wound photos, dental images, and endoscopies. The code that makes all this possible isn't elegant by today's standards, but it is stable, time-tested, and works just the way someone trying to practice state-of-the-art medicine would want it to work. "The beauty of VistA," says Kreis, "is certain parts of it were not engineered in the early days in the classic top-down kind of design; it was more of a bottom-up design. What it may have lost in its engineering, it gained in its relevance."

FOUR

VistA in Action

Today, one can see the legacy of the Hard Hats' triumph by visiting the Washington VA Medical Center. It's an imposing structure located three miles north of the Capitol building. When it was built in 1972, it was in the heart of Washington's ghetto, and as one nurse told me, she used to lock her car doors and drive as fast as she could down Irving Street when she went home at night.

Today, the surrounding area is gentrifying rapidly, and the medical center, too, is not what it once was. Certain sights, to be sure, remind you of how alive the past still is here. In its nursing home facility, there are still, as of this writing, a few veterans of the Great War. Standing outside of the hospital's main entrance, I was moved by the sight of two elderly gentlemen, both standing at near attention and sporting neatly pressed Veterans of Foreign Wars dress caps with MIA/POW insignias. One recounted that he was a survivor of the Bataan Death March.

But, even with history everywhere, this hospital is also among the most advanced, modern health care facilities in the world—a place that hosts an average of four visiting delegations a week from around the world. The spacious lobby resembles that of a normal suburban hospital, with a food court, ATM, and gift shop. But once you are on the wards, you notice something very different: doctors and nurses wheeling bed tables down the corridors with wireless laptops attached. How does this change the practice of medicine? Opening up his laptop, Dr. Ross Fletcher, an avuncular, white-haired cardiologist who helped pioneer the hospital's adoption of information technology, begins a demonstration.

With a keystroke, Dr. Fletcher pulls up the medical records on one of his current patients—an 87-year-old veteran living in Montgomery County, Maryland. Normally, sharing such records with an outsider would, of course, be highly unethical and illegal, but the patient, Dr. Fletcher explains, has given him permission.

Soon it becomes obvious why this patient feels that it is important to get the word out about the VA's information technology. Up pops a chart showing a daily record of his fluctuating weight over a several-month period. The data for this chart, Dr. Fletcher explains, flow automatically from a special scale the patient uses in his home that sends a wireless signal to a modem.

Why is the chart important? Because it played a key role, Fletcher explains, in helping him to make a difficult diagnosis. While recovering from Lyme disease and a hip fracture, the patient began periodically complaining of shortness of breath. Chest X-rays were ambiguous and confusing. They showed something amiss in one lung but not the other, suggesting possible lung cancer. But Dr. Fletcher says he avoided having to pursue that possibility when he noticed a pattern in the graph generated from the patient's scale at home.

It showed that the patient had gained weight around the

time he experienced shortness of breath. This pattern, along with the record of the hip fracture, allowed Dr. Fletcher to form a hypothesis that turned out to be true. A buildup of fluid in the lung was causing the weight gain. It occurred only in one lung because the patient was consistently sleeping on one side as a way of coping with the pain from his hip fracture. The fluid in the lung indicated the patient was in immediate need of treatment for congestive heart failure, and, fortunately, he received it in time.

Laptop Medicine

VistA is also an invaluable tool in managing chronic diseases such as cancer. "In the field of oncology," explains Dr. Steven Krasnow, the hospital's chief oncologist, "following blood counts of patients over time is very important. And the ability to essentially click one box and show a graph of the patient's individual blood count has been invaluable in maintaining patient safety and providing guidance to the clinician."[1]

VistA also plays a key role in preventing medical errors. Kay J. Craddock, who spent most of her twenty-eight years with the VA as a nurse and who today coordinates the use of the information systems at the Washington Veterans Affairs Medical Center, explains how. In the old days, pharmacists did their best to decipher doctors' handwritten prescription orders, while nurses, she says, did their best to keep track of which patients should receive which medicines by shuffling three by five cards.

Today, by contrast, doctors enter their orders into their laptops and the computer system immediately checks any order against the patient's records. If the doctors working with a patient have prescribed an inappropriate combination of medicines or overlooked the patient's previous allergic reaction to a drug, the computer sends up a red flag and prevents the doctor from continuing until the concern is acknowledged. Later, when hospital pharmacists fill those prescriptions, the computer system generates a bar code that goes on the bottle or intravenous bag. This bar code registers what the medicine is, whom it is for, when it should be administered, in what dose, and by whom.

Meanwhile, each patient and nurse has an ID bracelet with a bar code. Before administering any drug, nurses must first scan the patient's ID bracelet, then their own, and then the barcode on the medicine. If the nurse has the wrong patient or the wrong medicine, the computer will provide a warning. The computer will also create a report if a nurse is late in administering a dose, "and saying you were just too busy is not an excuse," says Craddock.

Craddock cracks a smile when she recalls how nurses first reacted to the system. "One nurse tried to get the computer to accept her giving an IV, and when it wouldn't let her, she said, 'You see, I told you this thing is never going to work.' Then she looked down at the bag." She had confused it with another, and the computer had saved her from a career-ending mistake—not to mention possible lethal harm to the patient. Today, says Craddock, some nurses still insist on getting paper printouts of their orders, but almost all applaud the computer system and its protocols. "It keeps them from having to run back and forth to the nursing station to get the information they need, and by keeping them from making mistakes, it helps them to protect their license." The VA has now virtually eliminated dispensing errors.

Speak to the young interns and residents at the Washington VA Medical Center and you soon realize that the computer system is also a great aid to efficiency. At the university hospitals where they had trained, they constantly had to run around trying to retrieve records—first upstairs to get X-rays from the radiology department, for example, or downstairs to pick up lab results. By contrast, when making their rounds at the Washington VA Medical Center, they just flip open their laptop when they enter a patient's room. In an instant, they pull up all the patient's latest data, and a complete medical record going back as far as the mid-1980s, including records of any care performed in any other VA hospital or clinic.

Along with the obvious benefits this brings in making diagnoses, it means that residents don't face impossibly long hours dealing with paperwork. "It lets these twenty-somethings go home in time to do the things twenty-somethings like to do," says Craddock. One neurologist practicing at both Georgetown University Hospital and the Washington Medical Center reports he can see as many patients in a few hours at the veterans hospital as he can all day at Georgetown. I couldn't help but wonder if Robin and I might have experienced fewer mixups and better access to her doctors at Georgetown's hospital if they had had access to a program like VistA.

By the time you read this, individuals enrolled in the VA will be able to access their own complete medical records from a home computer or give permission for others to do so. "Think what this means," says Dr. Robert M. Kolodner, acting chief health information officer for the VA. "Say you're living on the West Coast, and you call up your aging dad back East. You ask him to tell you what his doctor said during his last visit and he mumbles something about taking a blue pill and a white one. Starting this summer, you'll be able to monitor his medical record, and know exactly what pills he is supposed to be taking." Through the My HealtheVet website (http://www.myhealth.va.gov), which is integrated with VistA, vets are already able to refill prescriptions and keep track of personal health information, such as blood pressure and blood sugar readings. They will also soon have the ability to make appointments online.

VistA also reminds doctors about patients who need to make appointments and what medications they need. For example, it keeps track of which vets are due for a flu shot, a prostate or breast cancer screen, or other follow-up care—a task that is virtually impossible to accomplish using paper records. Today, the VA estimates that VistA has saved 6,000 lives by improving rates of pneumonia vaccination among veterans with emphysema and cutting pneumonia hospitalizations in half, thereby reducing costs by $40 million per year. At the same time, because VistA was written by VA personnel themselves, the VA pays no royalties for its use. Its total cost per patient comes to a mere $80.[2]

Another benefit of electronic records became apparent in 2005 when drug maker Merck announced a recall of its popular arthritis medication, Vioxx. The VA was able to identify which of its patients were on the drug, literally within minutes, and to switch them to less dangerous substitutes within days.

That same year, in the midst of a nationwide shortage of flu vaccine, the system also allowed the VA to identify, almost instantly, which veterans were in greatest need of receiving a flu shot and to make sure they got one. One aging relative of mine—a man who has had cancer and been in and out of nursing homes—wryly reports that he beat out 5,000 other veterans in the New London, Connecticut, area in getting a flu shot. He's happy that his local veterans hospital told him he qualified, but somewhat alarmed by what this implies about his health. During the 2004–05 flu season, 75 percent of all VA patients aged sixty-five and over received a flu shot, as opposed to only 63 percent of Americans in that age group who were not enrolled in the VA.[3]

The VistA system also helps to put a lot more science into the practice of medicine. Its electronic medical records collectively form a powerful database that enables researchers to look back and see what drugs and procedures work better than do others without having to assemble and rifle through tons of paper records. For example, using VistA to examine 12,000 medical records, VA researchers were able to see how diabetics were treated by different VA doctors, and by different VA hospitals and clinics, and with what outcomes. This allowed for development of treatment protocols based on hard data, rather than, as is often the case, on factors such as where a doctor went to medical school or on highly variable, local traditions of care.[4]

Wired for Science

VistA is also useful in identifying medical procedures that don't work, as well as particular doctors or surgeons who are not getting good results. For example, VA researchers have been able to use VistA's database of medical records to create the first national, risk-adjusted analysis of how patients fare after undergoing different types of surgery in different veterans hospitals. The study showed good news for the system as a whole. Between 1994 and 1998, mortality rates for major surgery fell by 9 percent, while morbidity rates, or the rate of complications after surgery, fell by 30 percent. But the study also quickly showed where outcomes were best and worst, thereby pointing to which surgical teams could stand as exemplars and which needed improvement.[5]

VistA's records can also provide important insights into the environmental factors behind disease and reveal important and otherwise overlooked correlations. For example, in October 2005, Dr. Fletcher, with a few keystrokes, checked to see how many patients in Washington Medical Center had blood pressure readings exceeding 140/90. The answer that came back was 45 percent. When he checked again in January 2006, he found that 50 percent had readings exceeding 140/90. Perplexed, he had VistA retrieve all blood pressure readings going back to 1998 and made an important discovery: blood pressures increase every winter and drop every summer. It's an insight that has important implications for how high blood pressure readings are interpreted and for prescribing appropriate medications. It has only come to light because of VistA.

VistA also makes it possible to track down new disease vectors with great speed and effectiveness. For example, when a veterans hospital in Kansas City noticed an outbreak of a rare form of pneumonia among its patients, its computer system quickly spotted the problem: all the patients had been treated with what turned out to be the same bad batch of nasal spray. VistA today plays a key role in the VA's avian flu surveillance program and allows for real-time data links with the Centers for Disease Control and Prevention—features that are likely to be invaluable in the event of bioterrorist attacks as well.

VistA has also proved invaluable during natural disasters.

When Hurricanes Katrina and Rita devastated New Orleans and the Gulf Coast in 2005, just about the only people whose health care records weren't gone with the wind or buried in mud were veterans enlisted with the VA, and it made a big difference. Floodwater swamped the VA hospital in New Orleans and destroyed its hospital in Gulfport, Mississippi. In all, an estimated 100,000 veterans in the area were forced to evacuate. But thanks to VistA's backup files, all patient records were preserved and within a hundred hours became continuously available through a special website accessible to VA medical personnel around the country. "So if the patient walked into any VA and said, 'I'm an evacuee from New Orleans,'" explains Terry Algood, chief of pharmacy at the Jackson Veterans Affairs Medical Center in Mississippi, "then that meant I could call into the Katrina Web site, look at the prescriptions, and then transfer those prescriptions into their database right there and take care of the patient on the spot."[6]

But it is not just information technology spawned by the Hard Hats that transformed the VA into what is now the nation's best-performing health care system. It also took shrewd and charismatic leadership from above to reengineer its culture and rationalize its processes. The story of the man who led that effort is one of the few truly successful examples of the Clinton era's many attempts to "reinvent" government. In essence, he succeeded by allowing the institution to take advantage of three of its unique features: its large-scale and deeply integrated information systems, its long-term relationship with its patients, and its comparative freedom from market-driven forces that in the private sector have impeded the quest for quality in health care.

FIVE

The Kizer Revolution

By the mid-1990s, the veterans health care system was in deep political crisis. Thanks to the triumph of the Hard Hats, it was already emerging as a world leader in the use of information technology to improve the practice of medicine. But a quarter of its hospital beds were empty.[1] One government audit in 1994 found that 21 out of 153 VA surgeons had gone a year or more without picking up a scalpel.[2]

It looked like what would finally undo the veterans health care system was the rapidly declining population of veterans. By the mid-1990s, World War II veterans were passing away at a rate of 1,000 per day. Moreover, those who survived in retirement tended to have migrated from the Northeast and the Midwest to the Sunbelt. This left veterans hospitals in places like Pittsburgh or on the Colorado plains with wards of empty beds and idle staff. Meanwhile, in places like Tampa and St. Petersburg, veterans hospitals were overwhelmed with new patients, who, facing overcrowded conditions and overworked staff, found plenty to complain about.

Adding to the threatening climate of opinion, some liberals as well as conservatives were beginning to ask questions about the veterans health care system that they would not have dared to raise at any other time in the twentieth century. "You mention the word 'veteran,' and you're supposed to pitch forward on your sword," Senator Alan K. Simpson, Republican of Wyoming and chairman of the Veterans' Affairs Committee, complained to the *New York Times* in 1994. He and other fiscal hawks increasingly saw spending on veterans health as just another wasteful form of pork barrel spending.

Meanwhile, serious voices on the other end of the political spectrum called for simply dismantling the veterans health system. Richard Cogan, a senior fellow at the Center on Budget and Policy Priorities in Washington, told the *New York Times* in 1994: "The real question is whether there should be a veterans health care system at all."[3] At a time when the other health care systems were expanding outpatient clinics, the VA still required hospital stays for routine operations like cataract surgery. A patient couldn't even receive a pair of crutches without checking in. Its management system was so ossified and top-down that permission for such trivial expenditures as $9.82 for a computer cable had to be approved in Washington at the highest levels of the bureaucracy.[4]

The major veterans service organizations, such as the American Legion, still supported the VA, but many individual veterans, especially younger ones, would use its hospitals only as a last resort. Hollywood once again captured and helped reinforce the public's negative perception of the VA with the movie *Article 99*, which was about a group of doctors in a veteran's hospital who had to contend with too many patients, budget cuts, and ruthless administrators.

Press reports, meanwhile, continued to serve up chilling anecdotes and damning conclusions. "The VA's War on Health" read a *Wall Street Journal* headline in 1993. "The Worst Health

Care in the Nation," the *Washington Times* echoed in 1994. It was a demoralizing time for those who still believed in the nobility of the VA's motto, which was, in words borrowed from Abraham Lincoln's second inaugural address "to care for him who shall have borne the battle, and for his widow, and his orphan."

Within the Clinton White House, skepticism about the veterans health system also ran deep. Early on in the first term, Hillary Clinton and other proponents of the administration's original health care plan had imagined that veterans hospitals might simply be folded into a much larger federally organized system of "alliances" they were planning. Even after their master plan crashed and burned in 1993, there were still many in the administration who questioned whether veterans hospitals ought to have a future.

Enter Ken Kizer

In January 1994, Kenneth W. Kizer, MD, MPH, was surprised to learn, if for no other reason than that he was a registered Republican, that he was on the administration's short list of candidates to head the Veterans Health Administration—a position that had remained unfilled since Clinton's election in 1992. He could hardly be sure at first what the administration might have in mind. "There were a fair number of people who thought the system wasn't salvageable," Kizer recalls today. "People in the administration; people out of the administration; the health policy wonks. You know, there were a fair number who just said no."

Yet his background, temperament, and intellect had given Kizer a unique vision of not only how to reform the veterans health system, but how to turn it into a model of twenty-first century health care—a vision that fortunately reached the administration's ears. In announcing his new VA undersecretary for health, the president enthusiastically noted that "Dr. Kizer brings a wide range of clinical and administrative expertise to the VA at a time when tested leadership will be crucial to the Department's success in the framework of national health care reform." It was a prediction that has become more true today than Clinton probably dared to imagine. Indeed, future historians may well record that among Clinton's greatest legacies was the reform of the VA, which transformed it from one of the biggest arguments against socialized medicine into one of the best arguments for it.

Kizer was idealistic enough about his vision that when he got the nod from the Clintons, he gave up a comfortable professorship at the University of Southern California, left his wife and kids behind, and threw himself into his new job. "Everyone said don't take the job. Or take it if you want to have yourself a fling in Washington, but don't delude yourself by thinking that you're actually going to be able to do anything," Kizer recalls. "There was universal consensus that if there was one agency that was the most politically hidebound and sclerotic, it's the VA. But what I saw, and what I thought the opportunity was, was that they had all the pieces."

Whatever else it was, the VA's health care system was a *system*, however ill-fitted its various pieces might be. It operated 159 medical centers around the country, 375 ambulatory clinics, 133 nursing homes, 39 domiciliaries offering care to the homeless and substance abusers, and 202 readjustment counseling centers. Moreover, it had a clearly defined base of patients with whom it maintained nearly lifelong relationships, thereby opening up the prospect of effective investment in prevention and disease management.

Kizer also liked VHA's clear mission—to keep patients healthy—and that it didn't have to maximize shareholders' profit or doctors' income. Also, because its mission centered on patients rather than profits, a core of VHA employees were highly idealistic and committed to improving quality. As Kizer saw it, the great opportunity lay in truly integrating this system and taking advantage of its potential, including investment in prevention, primary care, and highly coordinated, patient-centered, evidence-based medicine.

Kizer was not deeply experienced in the ways of the VHA, much less Washington. The Republican outsider, he was one of very few people to ever head the VHA who hadn't come up through its ranks. After his first day on the job ended at about 9:00 p.m., he found himself locked outside the VHA's underground parking lot and spent an hour pounding on doors trying to get someone to help him retrieve his car. When he finally did gain entry, he found his car vandalized. Weirdly, someone had stolen the headrests.

But Kizer was well prepared in every other respect. Orphaned at an early age, he had worked his way up through Stanford and the University of California at Los Angeles, becoming board certified in six medical specialties. His experience with military medicine included an internship at a VA hospital as well as service as a rescue diver in the navy reserves during the 1970s.

Adding to this background was Kizer's academic and professional experience in public health. He practiced emergency medicine early in his career but says he was frustrated by the limitations of having to care for one patient at a time. Hoping to take a more systematic and preventive approach to health care, he joined California's public health department in 1984 and rose through the ranks quickly. By age thirty-two he was appointed by California's Republican governor, George Deukmejian, to become the youngest person ever to head the department.

Developing the state's response to the new AIDS crisis was one of the responsibilities Kizer took on in that position. So was spearheading California's toxic waste cleanup efforts and early, antismoking initiatives. These included banning smoking for the first time in the public health department's own buildings, which proved sensitive. As it happened, California's public health department was highly unionized. It included sixteen different bargaining units, one of which represented its scientists. Another represented the blind vendors who sold cigarettes in the lobby. Kizer's experience negotiating with all these bargaining units would later prove invaluable at the VHA, whose workforce is represented by five different unions. But equally important was the cast of mind that accompanies a responsibility for the health of whole populations as opposed to one patient after another.

This cast of mind tends to see health care as a system, not just a collection of individual doctors treating individual patients. Thus eliminating medical errors becomes a matter not of finding a doctor or nurse to blame but of finding root causes of failure in a health care system's various processes and procedures, or the lack thereof. Similarly, this cast of mind naturally looks for data to answer basic questions that too often don't get asked in the day-to-day practice of medicine, such as which drugs work better than others for most people most of the time. Because they concern themselves with how health care works at the "population level," people grounded in the public health paradigm also tend to see health itself as overwhelmingly determined by environmental and behavioral factors. The "ecology" of health, in this view, includes obvious factors like smoking or lack of exercise, but also less obvious ones, such as how much patients become involved in their own treatment, or how integrated and coordinated is the care they receive.

By the time Kizer arrived at the VHA, he was well prepared to appreciate the potential of the new systematic and data-driven model of care that was already being made possible by the development of VistA. He was also well prepared to see the necessity of reorienting the VHA away from a system that emphasized acute care delivered in hospitals by specialists and toward one that put overwhelming emphasis on prevention and patient-centered management of chronic conditions. The declining population of veterans would force the VHA to undergo painful downsizing, but in Kizer's vision this change could also be the catalyst for implementing a new and profoundly more efficient and effective model of health care.

To achieve this vision, Kizer first had to deal with politics, starting with those of the VHA itself. "The basic thesis of the transformation, when I was talking about it to people within the VA, as well as outside . . . was that we have to able to demonstrate that we have an equal or better value than the private sector, or frankly we should not exist," Kizer recalls today. "That didn't necessarily go down well, at least at first. But as a taxpayer, why should I pay for a system that provides poor quality, is inefficient, wastes money, and that the customers don't like?"

Demonstrating the value of the system, both to himself and

to others, required formal measures or metrics of quality. By the 1990s, it had become a truism of American business that "you can't manage what you don't measure." But within American health care, at the time, systematic attempts to define, measure, and improve quality were highly unusual. The British, with their nationalized health care system, had a long tradition of systematically studying the actual outcomes of different medical procedures and systems, and acting on them. But in this country, remarkably few researchers even had the concept of what is today known as "evidence-based medicine," and their work was largely ignored by health care providers.

Nonetheless, Kizer insisted that the system measure itself against any and all benchmarks of quality for which consensus existed among health care professionals. The metrics were somewhat crude and often measured inputs or processes rather than outcomes, but they were better than nothing. What percentage of elderly male patients received prostate cancer screening, for example, and how did this compare with their counterparts in Medicare? How many diabetic patients received treatments based on "best practices"? How long did vets have to wait to get appointments? How often did medical errors occur, and what were their patterns? How did patient satisfaction at the VA compare with that of other health care systems?

Kizer combined such measures into a gimmicky but effective management tool he called the "value equation," which he formulated as Value = (technical quality + access + customer satisfaction + health care status)/(cost or price). Thanks to the continuing evolution of VistA and other reporting systems, obtaining the data for this measure of cost-effectiveness would become increasingly easier, but the answers were not always pleasing or expected. For example, while it turned out that the VHA was doing a respectable job ensuring that its few aging female patients were receiving mammograms, only about 1 percent of its elderly male patients were being screened for prostate cancer.

Right Sizing

Armed with his metrics, Kizer began leading the VHA toward its transformation. One big, unpleasant, and unavoidable agenda item was how to rationalize the VHA's excess capacity. Because of the changing demographics of the veterans population, and the shift to outpatient care, the VHA had scores of hospital complexes and other facilities that had to be closed for lack of patients. It wasn't only a matter of money, it was also a matter of safety. When surgeons pick up a scalpel only one or two times a year, they are bound to be out of practice, along with all of their operating team and nursing support.

To help deal with this problem, Kizer began contracting with private hospitals in areas where there were too few patients to support a veterans hospital. He would also push for expanding eligibility for health benefits to veterans who were neither poor nor needing treatment for service-connected disabilities. Yet these steps were still not enough to maintain a safe volume of care at many VA hospitals. In some extreme examples, such as the veterans hospital in Grand Island, Nebraska, the average daily census of patients had dropped to just two.

A key to building enough political support to close such institutions was negotiating an unusual agreement with Clinton's

Office of Management and Budget. Under the agreement, any money Kizer managed to save by closing hospitals wouldn't simply go back to the Treasury, as under the normal rules of federal bureaucracy, but could be used by the VHA for other purposes, such as building new outpatient clinics, expanding VistA, or ensuring that every VHA patient was assigned a primary care physician. This allowed VHA employees, veterans, and other interest groups to see that much more was going on under Kizer's leadership than just ruthless downsizing.

Another key for cutting through political gridlock was Kizer's decision to push budget and policy making authority away from the VHA's central headquarters in Washington. As part of this decentralization plan, he created a series of twenty-two regional administrative districts, most of them overlapping state boundaries and vested with as much power as possible. One practical advantage was simply to put VHA managers closer to those they managed and thereby create more accountability. But the measure was also politically shrewd.

A U.S. senator like John D. Rockefeller IV of West Virginia, for example, who had particular leverage over veterans issues as chairman of the Senate's Veterans Committee, and who had a particularly contentious relationship with Kizer, found his state split up among five regional districts, all of which overlapped into other states. That was fine for West Virginia's veterans. Because of the state's mountainous terrain, people there have always been far more likely to travel to a neighboring state than to cross the state in search of care. But the administrative change meant that Rockefeller needed far more cooperation from veterans and politicians in other states if he wanted to save or tinker with some particular VA facility within his state.

Regionalizing the VHA power structure had other advantages as well, "It's easier to have that dialogue with real people in the community" says Kizer, "than it is with a congressional committee, where everyone wants to stand up for the flag and 'do something' for veterans, and you've got C-SPAN there hovering." Decentralization, combined with the VHA's state-of-the-art information systems, also meant that it became possible to hold regional administrators accountable for a wide range of performance measures, including how well they coordinated physician, hospital, and other medical care services for a defined population within their administrative region.

In his original blueprint for transforming the VHA, entitled "Vision for Change," Kizer wrote:

> In an integrated health care system, physicians, hospitals, and all other components share the risks and rewards and support one another. In doing so they blend their talents and pool their resources; they focus on delivering 'best value' care. To be successful, the integrated health care system requires management of total costs; a focus on populations rather than individuals; and a data-driven, process-focused customer orientation.[5]

Kizer presented this vision as an extension of trends that were already occurring in the private sector, which in the era before HMOs and "managed care" came to be vilified, was politically savvy. But in practice, Kizer's vision went far beyond any integration done by private sector providers, who quickly discovered that they most often lacked a "business case" for improving quality. In contrast to even the largest HMOs, the VHA could count on a relatively stable population of patients, which in turn gave it a built-in case for pursuing quality. Take, for example, the choice of drugs it uses. Many of those drugs, such as statins, which help lower cholesterol, bring about only long-term benefits to most patients—specifically, a reduced chance of one day suffering from heart attack or stroke. An HMO, in which patients are constantly churning, has no real financial interest in whether the particular statins it prescribes are the most effective, much less in whether its patients actually take their prescribed medicine.

For health care providers who lack long-term relationships with their patients, even the question of whether a drug may eventually turn out to have long-term safety problems is not particularly urgent, so long as it has been approved by the Food and Drug Administration. That's because by the time patients begin to experience any long-term complications, they will have long since moved on to other health plans. Because of the churning of patients that occurs in nearly every American health care system other than the VA, decision making tends to be dominated by short-term financial costs rather than by long-term benefits to patients' health.

Workhorse Drugs

Realizing the unique incentives the VA had to maximize its patients' health, Kizer set up an elaborate drug review process to establish what is known as a "formulary" of recommended drug therapies. Field investigations by VA physicians and pharmacists compared the effectiveness of new drugs with current therapies, considered any safety concerns, and decided whether the VA should include these new drugs in its formulary.

One result was that the VA would sometimes pay for pricey drugs that typically were not covered by other health care plans, such as an expensive but effective compound used in the treatment of schizophrenia, and high-quality statins used to treat high cholesterol. "If you know you're going to have your patients for five years, ten years, 15 years, or life," explains Kizer, "there are both good economic and health reasons why you would want to use these more expensive drugs. You have a population of patients who are at high risk for sclerotic heart disease, and, you got them for life. You make a different decision about what's on your drug formulary than you might if you knew you only had them for a year or two."

After evaluating the safety and effectiveness of different competing therapies, the VA typically settles on a few "workhorse" drugs—such as the statin simvastatin to treat high cholesterol—that become part of the VA's standard medical protocol. This exercise in evidence-based medicine not only brings health benefits to patients but also has the effect of further leveraging the VA's already considerable purchasing power over drug companies, thus allowing it to negotiate deep discounts even on the highest-quality drugs.

Predictably, many drug companies hate the power the VA has over them. They fund studies claiming to find some inadequacy in its formulary, with the usual complaint being that the VA does not include enough "new and improved" drugs. One such study, for example, published by the drug-industry-funded Manhattan Institute, purported to find a two-month decline in life expectancy among VA patients because the VA formulary included a lower fraction of new drugs than those typically in use by the rest of the health care sector.[6]

Yet the independent and prestigious Institute of Medicine debunked the claim, finding that "the VA National Formulary is not overly restrictive."[7] As the millions of Americans who took COX-2 inhibitors to treat their arthritis, including the millions who took Vioxx and other dangerous new drugs have learned all too painfully in recent years, just because the Food and Drug Administration approves a drug doesn't mean it is a superior therapy, or even a safe one. It only means that in some short-run trials, usually financed by the manufacturer, the new drug proved more effective than a placebo.

According to William Korchik, a VA doctor who has participated in the VA's drug review process, another of its big benefits over the years has been avoiding dangerous drugs. "We took a tough stand on the [COX-2] inhibitors by not putting the drug on our national formulary and requiring prescribers to complete a risk assessment tool on each patient before a COX-2 inhibitor could be provided." Predictably, Korchik continues, "we were criticized up and down about our restrictiveness. But now I can say we were appropriately restrictive because there was not data [proving their safety]."[8]

By 1998, Kizer's shake-up of the VHA's operating system was already earning him management guru status. His story appeared that year in *Straight from the CEO: The World's Top Business Leaders Reveal Ideas That Every Manager Can Use.* Yet the revolution he helped set in motion at the VA was only beginning, even as the rest of the U.S. health care system fell deeper into crisis.

SIX

Safety First

Everyone understands that a good health care system needs highly trained, committed professionals. They should know a lot about biochemistry, anatomy, cellular and molecular immunology, and other details about how the human body works—and have the academic credentials to prove it. But these days, if you get sick with a serious illness, chances are you'll see many doctors, including different specialists. Therefore, how well these doctors communicate with one another and work as a team becomes critical. "Forgetfulness is such a constant problem in the system," says Donald Berwick of the Institute for Healthcare Improvement. "It doesn't remember you. Doesn't remember that you were here and here and then there. It doesn't remember your story."

Are all your doctors working from the same medical record and making legible entries? Do they have a system to make sure they don't collectively wind up prescribing dangerous combinations of drugs? Is any one of them going to take responsibility for coordinating your care so that, for example, you don't leave the hospital without appropriate follow-up medication and the knowledge of how and when to take it? Just about anyone who's had a serious illness, or tried to be an advocate of a sick loved one, knows that all too often the answer is no.

And it's not just doctors who define the quality of your health care. There are also all kinds of other people involved—nurses, pharmacists, lab technicians, orderlies, and even custodians. Any one of these people could easily kill you if they do their job wrong, or if their job is not properly managed with safety in mind. Modern hospitals may not produce catastrophic failures that kill thousands of people at a time. But doctors, nurses, and hospital technicians routinely deal with very dangerous technologies, including powerful drugs, that do kill thousands of Americans every year, albeit usually one at a time. Even a job such as changing a bedpan, if not done right, can spread deadly infection throughout a hospital. These jobs are all part of a system of care, and if the system lacks cohesion and quality control, many people will be injured and many will die.

Just how many? Nobody knows for sure, of course. One problem is a culture of cover-up that pervades health care. All individuals involved in medicine face a very real likelihood of being sued, or punished by their superiors, if they admit to even trivial mistakes. Given the can-do ethos of medicine, personal shame also causes many doctors and nurses to obscure mishaps or mistakes.

Then again, many of the accidents that occur in medicine go unrecognized by all involved. The elderly patient slips into dementia and eventually a coma; no one realizes that the proximate cause of her death was a pharmacist who misread a doctors' scribbled prescription. Another elderly patient succumbs to pneumonia. No one realizes that the proximate cause of the infection was an orderly who neglected to wash his hands.

But there is no doubt the number of medical mistakes is very high. In 1999, the Institute of Medicine issued a ground-breaking study, entitled *To Err Is Human*, which still haunts health care professionals. By reviewing hospital medical records, it found that up to 98,000 people die of medical errors in American hospitals each year.[1] Subsequent findings suggest that the study may have substantially underestimated the magnitude of the problem. For example, hospital-acquired infections alone, most of which are preventable, account for an additional 90,000 deaths per year.[2] In 2006, the IOM issued a new study that found hospital patients in the United States experience an average of at least one medication error, such as receiving the wrong drug or wrong dosage, every day they stay in the hospital.[3]

On top of this are all the errors of omission. For example, there is little controversy over the best way to treat diabetes; it starts with keeping close track of a patient's blood sugar levels. Yet, if you have diabetes, your chances are only one in four that your health care system will actually monitor your blood sugar levels or teach you how to do it. According to a recent RAND Corporation study, it's an oversight that causes an estimated 2,600 diabetics to go blind every year and another 29,000 to experience kidney failure.[4]

All told, according to the same RAND study, Americans receive appropriate care from their doctor only about half of the time. The results are deadly. In addition to the 98,000 killed by medical errors in hospitals and the 90,000 deaths caused by hospital infections, another 126,000 die from their doctor's failure to observe evidence-based protocols for just four common conditions: hypertension, heart attack, pneumonia, and colorectal cancer.

Why does this extraordinary loss of life go on year after year? The short answer is that, with the large exception of the veterans health care system, few health care providers are integrated or cohesive enough in their management and operations to promote safety and evidence-based medicine systematically.

In health care as in all realms of life, the root cause of most accidents is not that some single person or even group of persons made a mistake, though they may have. Instead, the root cause is almost always a lack of any system or process for preventing human error or negligence. So, for example, a nurse may inadvertently kill a patient when she administers a dose of potassium chloride concentrate thinking that it is liquid Tylenol or saline solution. But the root cause of the mistake was not the nurse's lack of diligence, though she may have been tired and distracted at the time. The root cause was the fact that both bottles were made by the same manufacturer and looked alike, and there was no system for preventing a nurse from confusing them. Because of this, firing the nurse won't prevent the accident from happening again, or even reduce its chances by much. Some other nurse will eventually also be tired and distracted and will make the same mistake until there is some systematic fix that prevents it.

Full Disclosure

Long before studies like *To Err Is Human* began to appear, the veterans health system under Ken Kizer had begun to attack safety issues systematically. His first step was to convince his boss, the late VA secretary Jesse Brown, that the VA should adopt a policy of full disclosure of any medical errors. Without this policy, Kizer argued, he could not get VA doctors and other personnel to see the scope of the problem or enlist them in creating a culture of safety.

The idea carried obvious political risk. No other health care provider in the United States disclosed its mistakes. Kizer quotes Brown as warning him, "If this goes south, and politically it doesn't work out, you're the first casualty." Kizer accepted those terms and announced the policy. Starting in 1997, the VA began maintaining a so-called Patient Safety Event Registry. Reporting of medical mistakes became mandatory. At the same time, the VA promised medical personnel that it was looking for systematic solutions to safety problems, not seeking to fix blame on individuals except in the most egregious cases. The good news was a thirty-fold increase in the number of medical mistakes and adverse events that got reported. The bad news was that those numbers, despite evidence of continued underreporting, added up to appalling totals.

According to a report released by the VA's medical inspector, the veterans health system committed 2,927 medical errors leading to 710 deaths between just June 1997 and December 1998. In addition to medication errors, the problems described by the report included surgery on the wrong body part or the wrong patient, errors in blood transfusions, patient abuse, improper insertion of catheters or feeding tubes, and a variety of other therapeutic misadventures. Other errors included losing track of 113 patients who turned up in hospitals and nursing homes in which they were not listed, and failing to prevent 277 patient suicides.[5]

It took a while for the press to catch wind of this report, though it was a matter of public record. Kizer remembers going to Kinko's one weekend to make a copy for the *New York*

Times's Robert Pear, who had called him at home to ask about its existence. Predictably, once Pear broke the story, it generated tough headlines around the country. "VA Finds Deadly Errors at Hospitals," trumpeted the *Orlando Sentinel*. Under the headline, "Killer Hospitals," the *Detroit News* editorialized: "Congress should disband the veterans health system and hand its beneficiaries vouchers or tax credits to purchase their own health care."

But many news outlets realized the broader context. The Institute of Medicine's well-publicized *To Err Is Human* report, released shortly before, gave every reason to believe that the rate of medical errors was even worse throughout the rest of the American heath care system. The VA was at least admitting to its own mistakes, and even more impressively, doing something about them. A positive *New York Times* editorial quoted the nation's top expert in health care safety, Dr. Donald Berwick: "The Veterans Health Administration has made a more serious commitment to improving health safety than any other large system in the country."

Lessons from *Challenger*

Among the signs of that commitment was Kizer's recruitment of former air force flight surgeon, astronaut, and NASA accident investigator James P. Bagian to head up a new National Center for Patient Safety, based in Ann Arbor, Michigan. Bagian, who supervised NASA's investigation of the 1986 *Challenger* space shuttle disaster, brought with him the view that safety can only be achieved by creating systems that are, as he puts it, "fault tolerant." O-rings and other tiny parts will fail; the challenge is to find out why and when they do, and to engineer changes that minimize the consequences. Similarly, some managers will always be tempted to discount safety concerns; the challenge is to build management processes that put the burden of proof on those who argue that a flight is safe to launch rather than on those who have doubts. At the same time, "close calls" and "near misses" will happen far more than actual accidents. The challenge here is to make sure there are processes by which as many as possible get reported and analyzed so that their root causes can be determined and future catastrophes avoided.

Such precepts have long been recognized in the world of aviation, but no one had ever attempted to apply them systematically to the world of health care. Among Bagian's key moves was to set up a system, similar to those that exist within aviation, whereby VA personnel could report mistakes and near misses anonymously. Given how often medical personnel not only fear blame but also feel shame when they make a mistake, the measure was essential to gathering enough data to see the patterns that were threatening safety.

Many of these patterns involve highly technical procedures that are difficult to describe in lay terms, but others are straightforward and easy to understand. For example, most people have heard about surgeons who operate on the wrong organ or limb. It happened most famously to comedian Dana Carvey, when a surgeon unclogged the wrong artery and sent Carvey's career into a tailspin. So-called wrong site surgery happens in about one out of 15,000 operations, with foot and hand surgeons being particularly likely to make the mistake. Most hospitals try to deal with this risk by having someone use a magic marker to show the surgeon where to cut. But about a third of the time, Bagian's safety team has found, the root problem isn't that someone mixed up left with right; it's that the surgeon is not operating on the right patient. How do you prevent that?

Obviously, VistA helps a lot. Just scan the patient's ID bracelet and see what surgical orders come up on the computer screen. That's one big reason why the VHA's rate of wrong-site surgery has long been far below that of the American health care system in general. But even VistA isn't foolproof. What if someone mistyped the orders or made a mistake in coding the ID bracelet? Drawing on his previous NASA experience, Bagian developed a five-step process that VHA surgical teams now use to verify both the identity of the patient and where they are supposed to operate. Although it's similar to the check-off lists astronauts go through before blastoff, it is hardly rocket science. The most effective part of the drill, says Bagian, is simply asking the patient, in language he can understand, to state (not confirm) who he is, his birthdate or Social Security number, and what he's in for.

Another safety measure taken by Bagian was equally simple, and also an important lifesaver. Acting on tips from nurses, Bagian began noticing a significant number of instances in which patients were mistakenly injected with concentrated potassium chloride. This drug, which is normally used in diluted form to treat potassium deficiencies, is easily confused with sodium chloride (saline solution) or with liquid Tylenol, which comes in a similar bottle. The fail-safe solution: a policy of never allowing the concentrate to be stored in wards, backed up by barcoding of all medications.

Following in the tradition of the Hard Hats, this last measure, which is the single most important safety feature adopted by the VHA, was made possible by ordinary VHA employees acting on their own. While returning a rental car in 1992, a nurse in Topeka, Kansas, the late Sue Kinnick, noticed an employee using a handheld device to scan a barcode in the trunk of the car. A light went on. "If they can do this with cars, we can do this with medicine," Kinnick later told an interviewer.[6]

With only minimal funding and management support, Kinnick joined with pharmacist Chris Tucker and fellow nurse Russ Carlson to develop the necessary software and ran a pilot project in a thirty-bed gerontological psychiatry ward by 1994.[7] Kizer says that when he got wind of this during a network managers meeting, "I said 'Wow. That's pretty impressive. I need to see this.' I got on a plane and went out to Topeka. Spent a day there, walked through with them how they did it, and said this is something we need."

Kizer had good reason to be enthusiastic. The software virtually eliminated dispensing errors. Just within the VA's Eastern Kansas Health Care System, where it was first rolled out, it wound up preventing some 549,000 errors by 2001. There was a 75 percent decrease in errors involving the wrong medication, a 62 percent decrease in errors involving wrong dosage, a 93 percent reduction in the wrong patients receiving medicine, and a 70 percent decrease in the number of times nurses simply forgot or didn't get around to giving patients their meds.[8] At the time, there was no equivalent product available from the private sector, and even today, few hospitals outside the VA have automated their drug-dispensing systems. Meanwhile, after asking two outside consultants to evaluate VistA, Kizer had concluded that it, too, had no rival in the private sector and ordered its universal adoption. No longer would VHA physicians be allowed to handwrite prescriptions and keep notes exclusively on paper; they'd have to learn how to use VistA if they didn't already know. His decision wasn't greeted with overwhelming acclaim. Kizer estimates that between 5 and 10 percent of VHA doctors quit over the measure. But most, he says, were older specialists that the VHA no longer needed because of its new emphasis on prevention and primary care. Moreover, the promise of VistA was just too great.

Sue Kinnick's drug-dispensing software, for example, could easily be folded into VistA, and together they became a powerful tool for safety. VistA's electronic medical records take the guesswork out of whether a comatose or incoherent patient has a history of allergic reactions to penicillin or other drugs. Kinnick's computerized dispensing system, meanwhile, takes the guesswork out of what some other doctor might have meant (Celexa, Celebrex, or Cerebyx?) with a cryptic scrawl or mumbled tape-recorded notes. In short, all the programs that eventually became today's VistA, in addition to their many other virtues, became the "killer ap" for the systematic prevention of medical errors and quality improvement.

Bright Star

Of course, medical errors still do occur in the veterans health care system, and when they do, they are bound to make headlines. But when you see such a headline and wonder how safe veterans hospitals really are, the key question to ask is, Compared to what?

Writing in the *New England Journal of Medicine* in 2005, Harvard's Lucian L. Leape and Donald Berwick surveyed patient safety efforts throughout American medicine and came to rather dreary conclusions. They noted that there was no statistical evidence that the rate of medical errors was declining for the American health care system as a whole, and that there was plenty of reason to believe that new technologies and more powerful drugs were making it more dangerous.

They despaired that there still did not exist any comprehensive nationwide monitoring system for patient safety and bemoaned the widespread denial among doctors that safety was a problem in medicine. "Why has it proved so difficult to implement the practices and policies needed to deliver safe patient care?" they plaintively asked. "Why are so many physicians still not actively involved in patient safety efforts?" But amidst their gloom over lack of progress, they still saw hope in one shining exception.

"The Veteran's Health Administration quickly emerged as a bright star in the constellation of safety practice," they wrote, citing its systemwide implementation of safety practices, training programs, and investment in safety research centers. They concluded optimistically that the rest of American health care would eventually catch up to the VHA in its use of electronic medical records and wide diffusion of proven and safe practices.[9]

But as we'll see in the next chapter, this is not likely, barring very fundamental changes in the organization and financing of American medicine. The veterans health system operates under unique incentives. It makes no money by providing unnecessary or ineffective treatments or tests. Instead, by promoting its patients' long-term health and safety, it saves money while also gaining political support and funding. Its doctors also form a self-selected population of professionals who tend to worry less about maximizing their own income and autonomy than about pursuing a calling. In short, the VA operates under conditions that give it a case for quality—a case that the rest of the American health care system cannot make so long as it has little or no incentive to keep people well or make them better.

Who Cares about Quality?

The medical economist J.D. Kleinke makes a revealing comparison between casinos and hospitals. Suppose you go to Las Vegas and after winning a few bets get hooked. When you start losing, you find yourself going to the cage and converting all the money in your wallet into chips. Next you max out your credit cards. Later that night, with Lady Luck still flirting but denying you the big score, you convert your checking and savings accounts into still more chips. When these are gone twenty-four hours later, the casino happily lends you another $25,000 worth of chips, which represents 40 percent of your retirement account and 30 percent of the equity in your home. Then, sipping on yet another free scotch, you make one big last bet at the craps table and are suddenly struck by a massive heart attack.

An ambulance rushes you to the nearest hospital. What's different about your new location? For one, you've gone from an institution that knows lots about you and your past to one that knows practically, or maybe even literally, nothing. The casino, before it processed your credit cards or lent you money, used advanced but routine information technology to discover details about your life such as your current employer, whether you've been caught at or suspected of cheating in another casino, your bank account balances, whether there are liens on your house, and whether your life insurance is paid up. All it needed to retrieve these details was your name, Social Security number, and a modest investment in information technology.

But the hospital you arrive at clutching your chest has no ability to retrieve the information about your past that it needs to do its job—unless, of course, it happens to be a veterans hospital. Sure, a clerk can check out your insurance status by telephone, assuming you're conscious or remembered to carry your insurance card. A clerk can maybe even find out if you've met your deductible, assuming the insurance company's computers are "up." But outside the VA, only a handful of hospitals has made the investment necessary to retrieve electronically, even from its own records, the name of your primary care physician, for example, or what medications you're on, your history of allergic reactions to various drugs, or even the name of your next of kin. Nor can most health care providers even communicate internally without relying on hand-delivered, handwritten notes, so that when an emergency room doctor scribbles out a prescription for beta-blockers, you wind up getting, well, who knows what?

Casinos invest in information technology because it helps them with the business they're in, which is encouraging impulsive gambling. Similarly, banks have found a business case for creating a highly integrated and sophisticated network of ATMs, to the point that you can draw cash from your account across the country and around the world. Yet hospitals make no equivalent investment in information technology to help them with the business they are presumably in, which most people would say is restoring people to health. Instead, American hospitals routinely endanger their customers and kill hundreds of thousands of them by clinging to nineteenth-century information technology. The question is why?

Kleinke has an answer that is as rude as it is true. It has nothing to do with technological feasibility. As far back as the 1970s, as we've seen, amateur programmers working on VA word processors were banging out the code for the VA's proven health care information management system. Instead, Kleinke argues, the answer has to do with health care's dirtiest of many dirty secrets: "Bad quality is good for business. And the surest road to bad quality is bad or no information."[1]

Quality Doesn't Pay

If this strikes you as too harsh, take a breath and consider. With the exception of the VA, what do most health care providers get paid to do? Provide health? Hardly. They get paid to provide treatments, and there's a big difference. This is not to suggest that most doctors are simply profit maximizers or indifferent to your health. Many in all walks of medicine are profoundly idealistic and believe in providing the highest-quality medicine possible. But given the system under which they operate, there is only so much idealism they can afford.

That's because, as Lawrence P. Casalino, a professor of public health at the University of Chicago, puts it, "The U.S. medical market as presently constituted simply does not provide a strong business case for quality."[2]

Casalino speaks from his own past experience as a solo practitioner and on the basis of over 800 interviews he has since conducted with health care leaders and corporate health care purchasers. While practicing medicine in Half Moon Bay,

California, Casalino had an idealistic commitment to following emerging best practices in medicine. That meant spending lots of time educating patients about their diseases, arranging for careful monitoring and follow-up care, and trying to keep track of which prescriptions and procedures various specialists might be ordering.

Yet Casalino quickly found out that his commitment to quality wasn't sustainable, given the rules under which he was operating. Nobody paid him for the extra time he was spending with his patients. He might have eased his burden by hiring a nurse to assist with all the routine patient education and follow-up care that was keeping him at the office too late. Or he might have teamed up with other providers in the area and invested in computer technology that would have allowed them to offer the same coordination of care found in veterans hospital and clinics today. Both steps would have improved patient safety and added to the quality of care he was providing. But even had he managed to pull them off, he stood virtually no chance of seeing any financial return on such investments. As a private practice physician, he got paid for treating patients, not for keeping them well or helping them to recover faster.

The same problem exists across all health care markets, and it's a major factor in explaining why the VHA has a quality performance record that exceeds that of private-sector providers. For example, suppose a privately managed care plan follows the VHA example and invests in a computer program to identify diabetics and keep track of whether they are getting appropriate follow-up care. The costs are all up front, but the benefits may require twenty years to materialize. And by then, unlike in the VHA system, the patient will likely have moved on to some new health care plan. As the chief financial officer of one health plan told Casalino: "Why should I spend our money to save money for our competitors?"

Or suppose an HMO takes a more idealistic attitude and decides to invest in improving the quality of its diabetic care anyway. Then not only will it risk seeing the return on that investment go to a competitor, but it will also face another danger. What happens if word gets out that this HMO is the best place to go if you have diabetes? Then more and more costly diabetic patients will enroll there, requiring more premium increases, while its competitors enjoy a comparatively large supply of low-cost, healthy patients. That's why, Casalino says, you never see a billboard with an HMO advertising how good it is at treating one disease or another. Instead, HMO advertisements generally show only healthy families.

Indeed, any health care provider in the private sector that holds itself out as providing high-quality care for chronic conditions risks financial ruin. That's a lesson Beth Israel Medical Center in Manhattan learned after it opened a new diabetic center in March 1999. To publicize the new venture, Beth Israel convinced a former Miss America, Nicole Johnson Baker, herself a diabetic, to pose for promotional pictures wearing her insulin pump. She also posed next to a man dressed as a giant foot, a dark reminder of how poorly managed diabetes often leads to amputation.

To avoid that and other dire outcomes, such as blindness and renal failure, the new center adopted a model of diabetic care that rivaled the VA's in its quality. Highly coordinated teams taught patients how to check their blood sugar levels, count calories, and find the discipline to exercise, all while undergoing prolonged and careful monitoring. Within months, the center succeeded in getting the blood sugar levels of 60 percent of its patients under control—a stunning result that brought it national attention.

But the idealists who conceived this program forgot the business they were in. Health insurers would pay only piddling amounts to cover the cost of a diabetic patient seeing a podiatrist, for example, though such care is essential to reducing the risk of amputation. And insurers would pay even less for nutrition counseling, much less exercise classes. At the same time, as word of the center's excellence in diabetic care spread, patient volumes increased by 20 percent a month. Soon the center was running a large deficit, and Beth Israel administrators felt compelled to shut it down. Between 1999 and 2006, three similar centers in New York based on the same model of care folded, and for the same reason. Quality doesn't pay.[3]

It's a similar story when it comes to the management of other major chronic conditions. For example, in 1995, Duke Medical Center had the bright idea of offering an integrated, supportive program for patients with congestive heart failure. Nurses regularly called patients at home to monitor their well-being and to make sure they took their medications. Nutritionists offered heart-friendly diets. Doctors shared data about their patients and developed evidence for what treatments and dosages had the best results. And it worked—at least in the sense that patients became healthier. The number of hospital admissions declined, and patients spent less time in the hospital. Only problem: by 2000, the hospital was taking a 37 percent hit in its revenue due to the decline in admissions and the absence of complications.[4] Ten hospitals in Utah had a similar experience after implementing integrated care for pneumonia.[5]

In many other realms of health care outside the VA, no investment in quality goes unpunished. Another telling example comes from rural Whatcom County in Washington State. There, idealistic health care providers banded together to form a creative "Pursuing Perfection" initiative designed to bring down rates of heart disease and diabetes. Following best practices from around the country, they organized multidisciplinary care teams to provide patients with counseling, education, and navigation through the health care system. They developed disease protocols derived from evidence-based medicine. They used information technology to allow specialists to share medical records and to support disease management.[6]

But there is a problem. Who will pay for it? The initiative is already greatly improving public health. It also promises to bring much more business to local pharmacies because more people are prescribed medications to manage their chronic conditions. It will also save Medicare lots of money. But estimates show that between 2001 and 2008, the initiative will have cost the local hospital $7.7 million in lost revenue and reduced the revenue of the county's medical specialists by $1.6 million.[7] One group of sixty doctors at the Madrona Medical Group of Bellingham took part in the planning but chose not to participate in the program when they realized how much the project would cost them. "We were seduced by the concept," Erick Laine, Madrona's chief executive, told the New York Times, "but it doesn't work." An idealistic commitment to best practices in medicine doesn't pay the bills. Today, the initiative survives only by attracting philanthropic support and, more recently, a $500,000 grant from Congress.[8]

For American health care providers outside the VA system, improving quality, more often than not, makes no financial sense. Yes, a hospital may have a business case for purchasing the latest, most expensive imaging devices. The machines will help attract lots of highly credentialed doctors who will bring lots of patients with them. The machines will also induce lots of new demand for hospital services by picking up all sorts of so-called pseudodiseases. These are obscure, symptomless conditions, like tiny, slow-growing cancers, that patients would otherwise never have become aware of because they would have died of something else long before. If you're a fee-for-service health care provider, investing in technology that leads to more treatment of pseudodisease is a financial no-brainer.

But investing in any technology that ultimately serves to reduce hospital admissions, like an electronic medical record system that enables more effective disease management, is likely to take money straight from the bottom line, however much benefit it might bring to your patients and to society. Because of its fragmented, market-driven system, the United States now lags at least a dozen years behind other advanced industrialized countries in its application of information technology to health care. Germany, for example, which began wiring its health care system in 1993, had spent $1.88 billion on its health IT system, or $21.20 per capita, by 2005, compared with 43 cents per capita ($125 million in spending) in the United States. Today, Germans carry encrypted "smart-cards," which they can use to let authorized health professionals retrieve their complete medical histories wherever in Germany they may happen to fall ill.[9]

The only exception to the generally laggard performance in U.S. health IT is the VA's VistA program. It's been installed in only a handful of American hospitals outside the VA, such as Midland Memorial Hospital in Texas. But it has been widely adopted by public health care systems abroad, including systems in Finland, Germany, Egypt, Nigeria, Mexico, India, Pakistan, and Uganda.[10] Dr. Ian Reinecke, the man in charge of Australia's program to bring electronic medical records to every citizen, has recruited VA officials to aid in the effort, explaining to his countrymen that "the US Veterans Health Administration is regarded as one of the best and most successful e-health systems in the world."[11]

Indifferent Employers

You might wonder why market forces don't drive the rest of the U.S. health care system to keep up with the rest of the world in the use of information technology. How is it that people in Uganda, Pakistan, and Mexico enjoy the benefits of VistA, but most Americans are stuck with doctors who use nineteenth-century information technology? Aren't Americans who buy health care concerned about its quality? If Toyota can win over customers and make money by selling quality automobiles, why doesn't some other company come along that does the same for health care?

It's not as if American consumers demand low-quality, dangerous, overpriced health care. If health care were like most other markets a Toyota of health care might well emerge in the private sector. But purchasers of health care usually don't know, and often don't care much, about its quality, and so private health car providers can't increase their incomes by offering it.

To begin with, most Americans don't buy their own health care; their employers do. How did this arrangement come about? It's not because most employers have, or have ever had, much financial interest in the long-term health of their employees, or even much stake in their short-term health—unless it involves an on-the-job injury for which they might ultimately have to pay.

Before government created worker's compensation, most employers invested little or nothing in their workers' safety, much less their long-term health. In 1907 alone, various explosions and accidents killed 3,242 American coal miners, while 4,534 railroad workers also lost their lives to workplace accidents. In 1911, when New York's Triangle Shirtwaist Factory caught fire, 146 immigrant workers perished because the owners kept the doors locked to prevent pilferage. It wasn't until progressives ranging from Teddy Roosevelt to Mother Jones at last won the fight for worker's compensation that anything like a safety-first culture began to emerge in American industry.[12]

So it is quite an irony of history that Americans ever entrusted their health, or their health care system, to the control of their employers, but that's what happened without anyone giving it much thought. America's employer-based health insurance system came about during World War II when the federal government imposed wage and price controls on the economy. To get around these wage and price controls, some companies started offering workers health insurance in lieu of raises.

Soon, the group health insurance business was flourishing. It managed to entrench itself further by winning generous tax subsidies, whose value increased as the burden of taxation borne by the rest of the economy grew. Even with these subsidies, however, it took a strong, and often militant, labor movement, and deep fear of Communism and "socialized medicine," to convince corporate America that it had better take responsibility for providing workers with health insurance. Today, as the labor movement fades in strength and militancy, fewer and fewer employers see any need to provide any health insurance at all, much less take interest in whether that insurance actually buys high-quality medicine. Today, only 59 percent of firms without union workers even offer health insurance, a share that declines year after year.[13]

Moreover, few employers have the wherewithal to secure high-quality health care for their workers even if they want to. A few large employers may have the staff and the market power necessary to evaluate the quality of different health care providers and to negotiate for greater commitments to patient safety and evidence-based medicine. And a precious few do, or at least go through the motions. For example, The Leapfrog Group, an industry-sponsored organization that presses for patient safety, has done some good work but suffers from chronic underfunding. The vast majority of employers have no interest in supporting such efforts and make no effort on their own to determine, much less change, the quality of the health care they buy on their workers' behalf.

The harsh truth is that most workers are not all that difficult to replace if and when they get sick. Sure, turnover costs employers, but not enough for them to take much interest in the long-term effectiveness of the health care their workers receive. Even for the very few workers who are truly indispensable, it makes no financial sense for their employers to spend money to help them put off or avoid, for example, the various chronic diseases of old age, because most of these workers will be retired or moved on to a new job before anyone realizes the benefit of such an investment. If it were otherwise, every company would have a wellness program to encourage exercise and proper diet. If it were otherwise, large employers would have long ago banded together and forced the health care sector to stop killing and injuring so many of their workers and inflicting others with poor-quality care.

Those, such as Harvard Business School professor Michael Porter, who believe pressure from employers will one day force health care providers to compete at "the right level"— that is, for value instead of price or cost-control—cannot explain why employers have not long since done so. It's a happy thought that healthy workers make for more productive workers. But the reality is that most people who meet a payroll don't think that goal is worth the cost. As a result, they either don't offer health insurance at all or remain little interested in the quality of care it buys.[14] Current trends in U.S. labor markets, which show wages and salaries accounting for the lowest share of GDP since 1947 even as corporate profits soar, suggest that most employers can get along just fine without improving the quality of health care their workers receive.[15]

Imperfect Information

You might also ask about employees themselves. Don't they care about the quality of their health care? Well, of course we do. But we either don't trust, or more often don't have, the information we need to determine, say, which hospital is safer than another, much less which individual doctor is more likely to perform unnecessary surgeries.

Most of us certainly know how to compare the nominal cost of different health care plans. And we can see how much different plans may or may not limit access to different specialists. But there is little we can tell about the quality of care those specialists and other doctors might provide, especially before that care is actually delivered, and often even afterward.

Recently, for example, the think tank at which I am currently a fellow changed health plans again, and I was forced to find a new primary care physician. Like most Americans, I've had to do this many times before, sometimes because I moved, sometimes because I changed jobs, and oftentimes because my employer changed health care plans in an effort to save money. So what did I wind up doing this time?

I make my living as a "knowledge worker." And I'm certainly no innocent when it comes to using government databases, NexisLexis, or the Internet. But none of those could provide me with anywhere near enough information to make a rational decision about which particular doctor might be better than another.

With a good deal of time, money, and know-how, you can usually figure out if a doctor has been sued for malpractice or convicted of some crime. You can also tell whether he or she is licensed and board certified. A very few insurance companies, as well as the Centers for Medicare and Medicaid Services, also allow their computer-savvy customers to glean some data on how much different doctors and hospitals actually charge for different procedures. If you know where to look, there are also websites that list doctors who are "gay and lesbian friendly," Christian, or African American, which is nice to know if such categories matter to you.[16] But as for any substantive indicator of any particular doctor's quality and performance, it's pretty much a shot in the dark.

I'm somewhat embarrassed to admit that the best strategy I could come up with in choosing a new doctor was to limit my search to those who were board certified, in group practices within ten miles of my house, graduates of medical schools I had heard of, and had websites. This last criterion may seem silly, but I hoped it would stand as an indicator of those comfortable enough with information technology to be likely to use electronic medical records.

My strategy worked, sort of. The one time I saw my new doctor he did come into the room with a laptop and was personable enough. He was even more or less on time. But the new commercial software he and his practice were trying to master allowed him to write me a prescription for blood pressure medication without indicating the dosage, much to my pharmacist's bewilderment and my own consternation.

And so we wind up making our choices in health based on factors like, "my best friend recommended this doctor," or "this doctor agrees with my diagnosis and refills the Ambien prescriptions I want." Or we use criteria such as, "I like this doctor's bedside manner," or "all the rich people in town go to this hospital." According to a recent survey, Americans spend twice as much time researching a car or computer purchase as they do selecting a doctor, which is not surprising given how little useful information there is to be had about any provider.[17] Those of us who are truly diligent might consult rankings of different hospitals such as those published by *U.S. News & World Report*, as Robin and I did when we needed to decide on a cancer clinic. But such surveys rely primarily on surveys of reputation—that is, on word of mouth—and give little weight to objective, statistical measures of quality. If they did, as we'll see in the next chapter, most of today's highest-ranking hospitals would be revealed as among the nation's most dangerous and ineffective.

Not knowing how to judge the quality of care doctors provide, we place inordinate value on our ability to change doctors. If one disappoints us for whatever reason, we can move on to another. Indeed, it's a sad irony that "choice of doctor" has become in most Americans' minds the single greatest measure of the quality of any health care plan. For it is the poor quality and fragmentation of the U.S. health care system that is ultimately both the cause and the consequence of our insistence on choice above all else.

And thus we see results like what happened in Cleveland during the 1990s. There, a well-publicized initiative sponsored by local businesses, hospitals, and physicians identified several hospitals as having significantly higher than expected mortality rates, longer than expected length of hospital stay, and worse patient satisfaction. Yet not one of these hospitals ever lost a contract because of its poor performance.[18] To the employers buying health care in the community, and presumably their employees as well, cost and choice counted for more than quality and safety. Unfortunately, as we'll see in the next chapter, the cost of this market failure in money, injury, and death can only rise as American medicine adopts more and more expensive, complicated, and often ineffective or dangerous technologies.

EIGHT

When Less Is More

Marjorie Williams died of liver cancer in early 2005, leaving behind a bereaved husband, two young children, and a network of loved ones and admirers who filled Washington's National Cathedral to the last pew at her memorial service. Her legacies are many, including a brilliant career as a political writer for *Vanity Fair* and columnist for the *Washington Post*. Yet she will perhaps be best remembered for her sharp and revealing descriptions, written near the end of her life, of her struggle with cancer, and about what it's like to be treated for it at some of America's very "best" hospitals.

In the first two and a half years of her illness, Marjorie received treatment from thirty-two doctors in six hospitals. She and her husband, Tim Noah, also an accomplished journalist and a friend of mine, were shrewd and well connected. They consulted with many medical luminaries in search of the very best care and treatments. And yet their quest for quality in health care was as disappointing as Robin's and mine.

"My most memorable brushes have been with an eminent surgeon," Marjorie wrote in her next-to-last column for the *Washington Post*, "whose method is to stride into the examining room two hours late, pat your hand, pronounce your certain death if he can't perform an operation on you, and then snap at your husband to stop taking notes, he can't possibly follow the complexity of the doctor's thinking." .

In the same column, Marjorie described another memorable moment on her journey.

> During one hospital stay, as I sat in a wheelchair outside Radiology waiting to be pushed back to my room, I began idly flipping through my chart. A young female doctor-in-training I had never seen before stopped in front of me and said, "You know, you really shouldn't be reading your chart." I thanked her for her advice and continued reading. She repeated her admonition. I explained that I was 43 and couldn't possibly read anything worse there than I had already been told by five real doctors. Upon which she actually wrested it from my grasp. (From this I learned always to go to a stall in the ladies' room when I want to read my chart.)[1]

Such anecdotes by themselves prove nothing. But Marjorie's experience helps us to visualize the reality behind a very odd truth in American medicine. Generally, the more prestigious the hospital you check into, and the more eminent and numerous the physicians who attend you, the more likely you are to receive low-quality, or even dangerous and unnecessary, care.

America's Worst Hospitals

The evidence for this assertion is as overwhelming as it is threatening to the medical establishment. The first hint of its truth came in the 1970s, when researchers John E. Wennberg and Alan Gittelsohn noticed strange patterns across regions in how doctors treated patients. By combing through old medical

records, Wennberg and Gittelsohn discovered wide and seemingly inexplicable differences in how often doctors diagnosed
people with peptic ulcers, for example, or in how often people
received such operations as tonsillectomies.[2] In the town where
Wennberg's kids went to school, Waterbury, Vermont, 20 percent of the children had their tonsils out by age fifteen; but in
next-door Stowe, 70 percent of the children got tonsillectomies.[3]

Differences in socioeconomic status could not explain the
contrast. Nor was it plausible to believe that the kids in Stowe
were far more in need of tonsillectomies than were kids in
Waterbury. The wide variation in practice patterns suggested
that something besides scientific rationality was at work in deciding which patients received what care—an idea that at the
time was as radical as it was novel. Doctors, after all, were supposed to be professionals who put their patients' interests before their own and who administered care according to the
dictates of science.

Gradually, Wennberg and other researchers, most of them
on the faculty of the Dartmouth Medical School, found clever
ways to tease out what was going on, and the emerging truth
was grim. For most Americans, the two biggest determinants
of what kind of treatments they receive are how many doctors
and specialists hang a shingle in their community and which
one of them they happen to see. The more doctors and specialists around, the more tests and procedures performed. And
the results of all these extra tests and procedures? Lots more
medical bills, exposure to medical errors, and a *loss* of life
expectancy.

It was this last conclusion that was truly shocking, but it became unavoidable when Wennberg and others broadened
their studies. They found that it's not just that renowned hos-

pitals and their specialists tend to engage in massive overtreatment. They also tend to be poor at providing critical but routine care. For example, Dartmouth researcher Elliot S. Fisher has found that among Medicare patients who share the same age, socioeconomic, and health status, their chance of dying in the next five years is greater if they go to a *high*-spending hospital than to a *low*-spending hospital. One reason is that patients in high-spending hospitals with lots of specialists and high technology are also *less* likely to receive many proven routine treatments.

For example, standard, evidence-based medicine has identified aspirin as a highly effective treatment for heart attack victims. Yet, in the highest-spending hospitals, only 74.8 percent of heart attack victims receive aspirin upon discharge from the hospital, as opposed to 83.5 percent in the lowest-spending hospitals. This may be one reason why survival rates for heart attack victims are actually higher in low-spending hospitals than in high-spending hospitals.

Patients in high-spending hospitals are also far less likely to receive flu vaccines (48.1 percent versus 60.3 percent) as well as such routine preventive measures as pneumonia vaccines, Pap smears, and mammograms. This general lack of attention to prevention and follow-up care in high-spending hospitals helps to explain why not only heart attack victims but also patients suffering from colon cancer and hip fracture also stand a better chance of living another five years if they stay away from "elite" hospitals and choose a lower-cost competitor. By doing so, they not only gain a better chance of receiving effective preventive and follow-up care, but they also gain a better chance of avoiding unnecessary and often dangerous surgery. Given this unexpected reality, it is perhaps not surprising that patient satisfaction also declines as a hospital's spending per patient rises.[4]

This isn't a statistical fluke. Sure, even among equally ill patients, those who are more aware of the risks of their illnesses may move closer to more prestigious and expensive hospitals. But, while that may be a small factor, the relationship between more money spent per patient and mortality exists among teaching hospitals themselves, even within the same region. And it also applies equally to patients who moved recently and to those who did not.

From evidence like this, Fischer estimates that if medical practice in the highest-spending hospitals could only be brought in line with medical practice in the lowest-spending hospitals, financial savings of up to 30 percent could be achieved in Medicare, thereby preserving the solvency of its trust fund indefinitely. And, not only would we have that happy result, but Medicare patients would receive less-dangerous and higher-quality care as well.[5]

Results like these have been repeatedly confirmed by a cascade of similar studies. Tellingly, doctors themselves seem to know instinctively the truth behind them. In 2006, when *Time* magazine had the brilliant idea of asking doctors what scared them most about being a patient, three frequent answers were fear of medical errors, fear of unnecessary surgery, and fear of contracting a staph infection in teaching hospitals.[6]

Now perhaps it becomes more evident why the VA's health system keeps coming out on top in measures of health care quality. Although the VA is exceptional in its use of evidence-based medicine, information technology, disease management, and root-cause approach to patient safety, its superior performance is also a measure of how fragmented and ineffective its competition is. America's medical elites are very good at attracting money and prestige, and they have a huge technology arsenal with which they attack death and disease. But they have no positive medical results to show for it in the aggregate and many indications that they are providing lower-quality care than the much maligned HMOs and assorted St. Elsewheres.

Roemer's Law

How can we possibly explain such strange findings? The beginning of all wisdom, when it comes to understanding the business of health care, is to understand that, in this realm, supply often creates its own demand. This of course seems counterintuitive and inconsistent with our experience. After you've waited two weeks to see a specialist, or to have a PET scan, it is hard to imagine that there is anything but an acute shortage of medical professionals and money to equip them.

But the real reason you have to wait to see a specialist is not that there are too few of them but that there are too many. Specialists who move into a community induce demand for their services just by offering them, even if their treatments provide little or no benefits, or indeed are harmful to most patients. For a similar reason, hospital beds are almost always full because their supply is so great. Add another hospital bed, and one way or another, the local health care system will find a way to fill it. The phenomenon is known as Roemer's law, after the late health care economist, Milton I. Roemer, who first described it in the late 1950s and early 1960s.[7]

There are two basic explanations for why Roemer's law arises. The first involves a short circuit in the normal way supply and demand adjust to one another. In most realms of the economy, demand eventually meets supply through changes in prices. If GM produces more cars than people need or want to buy, it winds up cutting prices and offering rebates until the cars are sold. Eventually, if GM can't cover its costs, it will make fewer and fewer cars, or even go out of business.

By contrast, health care prices don't drop when there is excess supply. One reason is because Medicare effectively controls health care prices. Whatever Medicare will pay for a procedure becomes the benchmark for what other insurers will pay as well. This might not be a problem if market forces determined Medicare's reimbursement rates for different procedures. But instead, it is a bureaucratic and political process that winds up setting rates and thus insures that whatever costs the health care system endures collectively are covered.

So the more capacity the health care system adds in the form of hospital beds, specialists, and high-tech equipment, the more money comes into the system. Some parts may wind up being more amply rewarded than others according to their success in influencing Medicare's rate schedules, but for the system as a whole, there is little or no check on excess supply. Instead, excess supply is absorbed through overtreatment and inefficiency. Under these conditions, it takes extreme mismanagement or a decline in the surrounding community before a hospital will ever go broke and shut down. If Medicare reimbursement rates prove insufficient to cover the cost of one kind of treatment a hospital offers—say, managing a diabetic's care—then a hospital can divert its resources to treatments for which reimbursement rates are more lucrative, such as heart surgery or chemotherapy.

The second reason Roemer's law applies is the stunning lack

of scientific knowledge about which treatments and procedures actually work. Doctors are highly trained professionals, and most are committed enough to their calling that they would never knowingly subject patients to treatments and tests that are straightforwardly and unambiguously excessive. The problem, however, is that medical textbooks are silent about what constitutes appropriate care for patients with many different illnesses, particularly for those nearing the end of life. For example, medical textbooks offer no evidence-based clinical guidelines for how often doctors should schedule such patients for return visits, when they should be hospitalized or admitted to intensive care, or what palliative care they should receive. Nor do medical textbooks offer clear guidelines, grounded in science, about when a doctor should refer a patient suffering from a specific condition to a specialist, much less when it is appropriate to order a diagnostic or imaging test.

And so we see results like the recent finding that the citizens of Elyria, Ohio, a small town near Cleveland, receive angioplasties at a rate four times the national average. It turns out that nearly all these angioplasties are performed by a group practice of thirty-one surgeons in town who have exceptional enthusiasm for the operation, perhaps because it is what they know how to do and it pays well. In the absence of any definitive protocols concerning the effectiveness or appropriateness of angioplasties, there is little or nothing regulators or insurance companies can do to crack down on even such obvious examples of overtreatment.[8]

And if the medical establishment is this much in the dark about what might be an appropriate way to treat your disease, where does this put you? It puts you in a spot where you can be very easily manipulated into just going along with whatever has become the customary way of treating your disease among the local medical community. Conversely, if you have made up your mind that you or a loved one should receive this or that operation, or should try out some drug you saw on television or the Internet, then you can probably find a doctor who will go along with your plans. Lacking clear guidelines about what appropriate care is, a doctor stands a very real chance of losing a lawsuit for refusing to offer some specific treatment or referral, especially if most other doctors in town routinely go along with it. At the same time, doctors, unless they're on salary, know that deferring to patient demands will put money in their pocket.

Other dynamics are involved as well. Patients learn from friends and neighbors that people who were struck by the same illness they think they might have went to Dr. So-and-So. For local hospitals, and health care plans, this means they must compete to get Dr. So-and-So on board, come what may. Except in the most extreme cases, no mere hospital administrator gets to point out that there is no evidence of Dr. So-and-So's treatments being effective or even safe.

In Our Lady of Lourdes Regional Medical Center in Lafayette, Louisiana, for example, there were rumors for years that one of its surgeons, a Dr. Mehmood Patel, was performing vast amounts of unnecessary heart operations. Yet it wasn't until one of Patel's fellow doctors at last secretly sued him in federal court under a special "whistle blower" law that the hospital revoked his admitting privileges. The hospital subsequently agreed to pay a fine of $3.8 million but still denies it had any way of knowing about the safety or effectiveness of Dr. Patel's care.[9]

As the number of specialists in a community grows, many

people cut out visits to their primary care physician altogether. Instead, they skip from one specialist to another according to what body part gives them reason to complain today, all the while gathering more and more bottles for the medicine cabinet. Dr. Alan Leshner, of the National Institute on Drug Abuse, estimates that 17 percent of Americans over sixty are abusing prescription drugs.

Many other patients are like "Peggy," an elderly woman profiled in a case study of the fragmented care typically delivered under Medicaid and Medicare. At age 83, Peggy went into mysterious decline, losing her appetite and eventually becoming so dizzy that she fell and injured herself in the bathroom. For a long time, she convinced herself and others that she was simply experiencing the natural consequences of aging. But when a worried son at last arranged for a comprehensive medical examination by her primary physician, it turned out she was taking four different arthritis medications prescribed by four different doctors. Embarrassed, she explained to her primary physician that she had heard of a few other doctors who were good at treating arthritis and sought them out.[10]

It's a common delusion that when one doctor or pill doesn't do the trick, maybe adding a few more to the mix will help one to feel better. As the supply of doctors and specialists increases, the culture of medicine becomes transformed. No longer is any single physician treating the whole patient, or taking responsibility for coordinating his or her care. As in extreme cases like South Florida and Manhattan, patients are seen by dozens of different specialists during the course of an illness or complaint, each of whom will happily make referrals to still more.

Over time, this pattern of care starts to seem normal to all involved. Some lonely elders even come to enjoy retelling their stories to different doctors or to those they meet in waiting rooms. It beats staying home and watching television. This fragmented form of medicine, which exists nowhere else in the world, might go on forever except that its financial costs are unsustainable, and its toll in medical errors, overtreatment, and neglect of prevention is, or ought to be, unacceptable.

What's Wrong with HMOs?

Roemer's pioneering work in documenting how supply creates its own demand in health care had a deep intellectual influence on the once idealistic movement to create health maintenance organizations. Today, many Americans view HMOs simply as organizations designed to make money by denying them care. And it's a sad fact that many HMOs have wound up doing just that, or else using clever marketing techniques to make sure they "cherry pick" only young and healthy customers who are unlikely to get sick. But it is important to remember that HMOs and other forms of managed care came into existence in large measure because of a big problem that is still with us and getting worse; namely, vast amounts of poorly coordinated, dangerous, and often excessive treatment.

The original vision of those who championed HMOs was that this form of care would vastly improve the quality of American medicine and only incidentally lower its cost. As Paul Ellwood, a pediatrician who more than any other single advocate built the case for HMOs, has said: "My own most compelling interest as a physician was in the integration of healthcare, quality accountability, and consumer choices based on quality first and, secondarily, price."[11]

In the late 1960s and early 1970s, doctors with a specific worry organized the precursors of what came to be known as HMOs. They saw the trend in medicine toward ever greater specialization, combined with the increasing prevalence of chronic disease in an aging, sedentary population, as requiring a far more systematic, integrated, and scientifically driven approach to health care. Specifically, they wanted an "integrated delivery system," in which "primary care" physicians would coordinate care in large, multispecialty medical group practices that would in turn be part of a system of hospitals, labs, and pharmacies. Moreover, to address the problem of overtreatment and lack of prevention, care would be prepaid. As Alain Enthoven, another champion of managed care, once wrote, this would give "doctors an incentive to keep people healthy."[12]

Already by this time, it was becoming apparent to those who studied the actual effects of modern medicine on the population as a whole that a new model of care was desperately needed. By the 1960s, the "crude" death rate, or number of deaths per 100,000 Americans, was no longer declining. Partly this was because the fall in birthrates since the end of the baby boom years meant that children and young adults constituted a smaller share of the population. But modern medicine itself was also a factor. Its very successes were causing a pandemic of chronic disease.

How, you might wonder? Up until right before World War II, it was a truism of medicine that, as the once famous medical textbook *The Principles and Practice of Medicine*, put it: "persons rarely die of the disease with which they suffer." Instead, secondary terminal infections, primarily pneumonia, carried off most patients with incurable disease, which is why pneumonia was once characterized by medical authorities as "the old man's friend."

Then, in 1937, for the first time in history, effective treatments for infection became available. These were the so-called sulfa drugs, and their introduction, followed by the discovery of even more effective penicillin and other powerful antibiotics, radically changed the way most people aged and died. Between 1936 and 1949, the death rate from pneumonia declined from just under sixty per 100,000 to just fifteen per 100,000. But this triumph of modern medicine came at a price. With the old man's friend and other secondary infections no longer carrying so many sick patients away, more and more people were left alive and still suffering from their primary disease while also bearing an increased risk for such chronic conditions as cancer, congestive heart failure, or the disease that came to be known as Alzheimer's.

The unexpected result was that the incidence of chronic illness exploded while mortality rates for the population as a whole stopped improving. By the 1970s, far-sighted researchers such as Johns Hopkins's Ernest M. Gruenberg started characterizing the rapid spread of chronic disease as examples of medicine's "failures of success." Modern medicine, in a quite literal sense, was enfeebling the population. Obviously, the answer wasn't to stop using antibiotics and other modern medical techniques. But the spread of chronic disease throughout the population did call for a new model of care.[13]

At the same time, the family doctor who made house calls and knew the circumstances of his patients was passing from the scene, and no one was taking his place. The family doctor may have carried in his bag little more than a stethoscope and various vials of opiates and alcohol, but the personal attention he paid to patients had huge, and by the 1960s, increasingly well-documented, curative powers.

Professor Kerr White showed in study after study how important an intimate and long-term relationship between doctor and patient was to health. Partly this was due to reasons you would expect, but White also found that much of the benefit of such a relationship came simply from "the placebo effect." The very presence of a familiar doctor laying on hands or writing a prescription gave patients hope and strengthened their will to live.

Also involved, White found, was "the Hawthorne effect." This was a phenomenon, already famous in managerial circles, that was first observed in the 1920s among women workers in a Westinghouse plant in Hawthorne, Illinois. During the course of a company study, the workers' productivity continuously increased under both good and poor working conditions. It didn't matter, for example, if they were forced to work in dim light or bright; the women kept on working harder so long as the study continued. Eventually, researchers could only conclude that the women were flattered that someone cared enough to pay close and careful attention to what their jobs were like. White demonstrated a similar effect in health care. He showed that patients in the care of a familiar and trusted physician are demonstrably more likely to modify their behavior—quit smoking, reduce drinking, take their medications—in ways that benefit their health.

Taken together, the placebo effect and the Hawthorne effect accounted for about half the benefits of all medical interventions, White showed. Armed with this insight, he went on to invent the concept of primary care and to pioneer the idea of an integrated or "managed" health care system centered on primary care physicians. The hope was that patients in the future would not simply get lost or be ignored as they passed from specialist to specialist.[14]

Such were the highly idealistic and data-driven concerns and issues behind the emergence of HMOs. This new model of care was specifically crafted to fit the changing nature of disease in the late twentieth century and to overcome the seemingly inevitable tendency of modern medicine toward specialization and therefore fragmentation. Cost containment was to be a happy, extra benefit of improved quality, safety, and effectiveness of care.

What went wrong? Eventually, HMOs morphed into many different forms and hybrids. Some were nonprofits, others were publicly traded companies answerable to Wall Street or large insurance companies. Some were "staff models" that put physicians on salary; others became little more than loose networks of doctors on contract. Some were run by idealists; others by shysters, crooks, and knaves. But they all had, and still have, one important common feature—a tenuous and short-term relationship with most of their patients.

By the 1990s, most people enrolled in any particular HMO had little or no choice in the matter; they were there because their employers were trying to save money. Nor, with few exceptions, could any single HMO expand into enough markets to hold on to its customers when they moved to other areas. The combined effect was to leave HMOs with no way to recover any investment they might make in their customers' long-term health.

It didn't help that many doctors felt threatened by the growing dominance of HMOs and other managed care providers and complained to their patients about it. Nor were the negative press and lawsuits that some HMOs attracted helpful to the industry's image. But what ultimately undid HMOs and true managed care was that, because of the constant churning of patients, they couldn't make good on their early promise to, as Enthoven put it, "keep people healthy."

With their economies of scale and aversion to overtreatment, HMOs could help keep prices down, or at least contain them better than traditional fee-for-service medicine. The overall rate of medical inflation fell sharply in the 1990s, thanks almost entirely to expansion of managed care. But because of their lack of a long-term relationship with their patients, managed care plans could not capture for themselves, nor for those they treated, the true value that this form of health care delivery potentially offered. Many went bankrupt. Many more responded by overscheduling doctors and discouraging access to specialists even when medically justified.

Yet as we move closer to examining the lessons the VA has to offer to the rest of the American health care system, it is important to remember that the problems that led to America's failed experiment with HMOs and managed care did not go away. Instead, they got worse, and will get worse still in the future.

Today, more than 90 million Americans live with chronic illnesses such as diabetes, cancer, and heart disease; and seven out of ten American deaths are caused by chronic illnesses. Population aging, combined with the sedentary habits of modern Americans and medicine's own "failures of success," will continue to increase the burden of chronic disease. On our current road, the human toll from medical errors will also increase as drugs become more potent and care becomes more fragmented. As the population ages, more and more people will also be killed by a health care system that fails to deliver routine preventive measures, such as flu shots, while neglecting or mismanaging chronic illness like diabetes. Finally, there are limits to how much Americans can pay for health care without ruining both their own finances and those of their country. HMOs are not the answer, most people would agree. Nor is the answer simply to create more subsidies so that more people can have greater access to a fragmented health care system that is grossly inefficient, ineffective, and unsafe. So what is the answer?

NINE

Battle Plan

The root cause of America's health care crisis is not a lack of market discipline. Indeed, when it comes to health care, market discipline has proven to be the disease for which it is supposed to be the cure. As currently constituted, the health care market repeatedly "disciplines" providers who try to improve the quality of their care and rewards those who do not. We have seen how private-sector hospitals that invest in electronic medical records, for example, or in prevention, or in management of chronic disease, run the risk of financial ruin under the current system, in which there is lots of competition, but mostly over price, not value or quality. And we have seen how market forces have at the same time led to vast amounts of ineffective and often dangerous overtreatment. At the same time, a large government bureaucracy has become the benchmark for quality, innovation, and cost-effectiveness in American health care. What are we to make of these facts, and what should we do about them?

Many readers may find the answer is obvious. The example of the VA, you may believe, just goes to show that a nationalized health care system modeled on the VA is a proven course for improving the quality of health care that all Americans receive. Yet

I imagine that many other readers will remain more skeptical. Even if they acknowledge the superiority of the VA model of care, they will doubt the political viability of extending it to every citizen. This is America, after all, and most Americans are instinctively distrustful of big government. Then there are all the massive special interests that have veto power over health care policy. Just look at what happened to Hillarycare.

Personally, I'm skeptical as well of any one-step government solution. You don't just wave a wand and create a whole new health care system, and if by chance you do, it's bound to bring all sorts of unintended consequences. There is an urgent need to reform the health care sector, but one needs to be politically shrewd in going about it. And so, for the remainder of this book, I lay out a strategy that will overcome the ideological objections and vested interests that have for so long prevented Americans from getting the affordable, high-quality health care they deserve.

Support Our Troops

The essential first step is a reform that is not only morally overdue but that also has the potential to bring great political advantage to members of either party who take it on as an issue. The first step is simply this: All veterans should have access to all the VA health care benefits they deserve and were promised when they enlisted.

Stop for a moment and look at America through the eyes of a younger veteran. Let's say you joined up on September 12, 2001, outraged by the attacks on the World Trade Center and the Pentagon. It was an emotional and impulsive decision, but part of what helped you make the case, both to yourself and to your loved ones, was the promise of future veterans benefits that would help make up for the sacrifice you and your family would be making.

One of these benefits, the recruiter enthusiastically told you, was that you would become eligible for VA health benefits *for life*, regardless of how much income you made or what illness or injury you might have. This recruiter wasn't exaggerating the promise made to veterans at the time. In signing the Veterans' Health Care Eligibility Reform Act of 1996, President Clinton himself explained that it "authorizes the Department of Veterans Affairs to furnish comprehensive medical services to all veterans."[1]

Now let's say it's five years later. Your tours in Afghanistan and Iraq are behind you. Your local community calls you a hero. Strangers offer to buy you dinner when they hear your story. You often see cars and SUVs with "Support the Troops" stickers. But there's a problem. Like one out of three veterans under the age of twenty-five (and more than one out of ten Gulf War veterans), you don't have any health insurance. The only job you can find doesn't offer it, nor can you afford to buy it on your own. And when you show up with all your papers in order at the local VA medical center, they tell you they're no longer allowed to care for you.

And why is that? Because it turns out that while you were fighting in the Middle East, Congress and the Bush administration conspired to repeal the "comprehensive medical services" you were promised by your recruiter and your nation. Now, unless you're living in poverty, VA doctors are forbidden to treat you any longer for "non–service connected" illness. What sort of country is this?

It is the sort of country in which, even during a time of war, veterans wind up losing vital, promised benefits, and it barely even registers on the national agenda. Specifically, as of January 7, 2003, the VA, having failed to receive the funding it needs to make good on the health care promised to millions of veterans, has restricted new enrollments either to those who can meet a strict means test or to those who have ailments directly and demonstrably related to military service.[2] This measure instantly disqualified most vets who are not already enrolled in the system from receiving VA health benefits. (Telling exception: all veterans of World War I and the Mexican Border War still have unrestricted access to the VA health care, provided they are still alive.) Even reservists who served in combat zones in Iraq and Afghanistan have access to VA health benefits for only two years following the end of their tour of duty unless they can demonstrate a service-connected disability or can meet the means test.

Bear in mind that this measure went into effect at the same time that Americans were rewarding themselves with the largest single expansion of health care entitlements in a generation: Medicare's prescription drug benefit. Remember, too, that the cutoff occurred while all Americans, and especially the well-to-do, were enjoying a series of steep cuts in federal taxes. Finally, consider that it happened at a time when the military was struggling to fill its enlistment quotas, and when the VA itself was being asked to dispose of dozens of underutilized hospitals around the country even as it was winning more and more praise from health care experts for its high quality. It's hard to imagine a more wrongheaded policy from any point of view.

Hidden Wounds

Aside from the moral objections, there are the practical ones. For example, forcing a distinction between service and non–service related conditions requires a huge bureaucracy, which must often make metaphysical judgments about what the ultimate causes of an illness or disability are.

Here's a real-world example decided by the Board of Veterans Appeals. A Vietnam veteran awarded the Purple Heart and many other medals in recognition of his action in combat presented himself to the VA in 1996 complaining of hearing loss. Records show that upon his discharge from the military, his hearing checked out fine, but that he has been using a hearing aid since 1992. Is the hearing loss the result of exposure to loud noise during the near daily firefights in Vietnam, in which case he is entitled to access to the VA health system? Or is it the result of the rock concerts he may have attended as a youth, or a natural consequence of aging, or some combination of all three?[3] You can imagine how many bureaucrats, lawyers, judges, and doctors are involved in determining such cases. The Board of Veterans Appeals hears some 38,000 cases a year, a huge portion of them involving disputes of this nature.[4]

Then there's the effect on the taxpayers. One big, real-world consequence of the tight eligibility rules currently imposed on the VHA is a far bigger bill from Medicare. "I do not understand the logic," says Ken Kizer.

> The VA is providing superior care, on a regular basis, than Medicare. Patient satisfaction is higher. You can show that it is doing it at a cost [per patient] of about half to two-thirds of Medicare. So why do you cut off people, tell them they

can't go to the VA, and force them into Medicare? And why do you not allow Medicare patients to use their benefits at the VA?

According to an estimate by the Congressional Budget Office, restoring full eligibility to the VA health system for all veterans starting in 2007 would save Medicare a total of $29.5 billion through 2015. Savings to the Medicaid program would come to $4.8 billion. Gains to society, though not calculated by CBO, would be much higher as millions of veterans escape the dangers of being uninsured or of being subjected to the fragmented care and overtreatment they currently receive outside the VA.

So step one on the road to solving America's health care crisis is simply to give veterans what they've been promised. After netting out the savings to Medicare, Medicaid, and other government health care programs, CBO projects that the cost would be about $38 billion in the first year and about $72 billion annually by 2015.[5] The real cost is much lower; indeed, the measure would free up society's resources for more productive use since the VA's cost per patient is lower than Medicare's and its care is more effective.

Diabetics under Medicare, for example, are far more likely to wind up requiring expensive amputations and dialysis than diabetics under the care of the VA—a consideration the CBO does not take into account when making its cost projections. Nor does the CBO consider how breaking promises to veterans drives up the cost of recruiting new soldiers, sailors, airmen, and marines. According to the Harvard/Cambridge Hospital Study Group on Veterans' Health Insurance, 1.7 million men and women who served their country have no health cov-

erage.[6] What message does that send to young people considering joining the military?

And it's not as if such a step involves impossible politics.
What conservative believes that our military isn't weakened
when America breaks its promises to veterans? What liberal
believes that showing solidarity with veterans and offering to
restore health benefits cut under the Bush administration isn't
politically shrewd? What American of any political stripe believes it's right to deny veterans benefits they were promised
when they signed up, especially for what has turned out to be
one of the longest periods of continuous combat in American
history?

Family Medicine

The same logic leads to step two on the road to comprehensive
health reform. It is to assure veterans, both young and old, that
their spouse and dependent children can also join an expanding veterans health care system. Ken Kizer, who knows a thing
or two about veterans politics and veterans health care, believes
that veterans would be "immensely pleased" by such a measure. And it would also go a long way toward improving the
quality of their care. It would allow, for example, an aging male
veteran and his wife to be treated by a single primary care
physician, who could deal with their codependencies and help
them to manage each other's various chronic conditions. What
the VA has been doing for the husband—that is, provide the
highest-quality, most cost-effective care in the United States—it
can do even better for the husband and wife together.

Or take an example from the other end of life. Under current law, the VA may provide medical benefits to a woman

during pregnancy and labor, but not to her baby. About 1,000 female veterans a year are forced to seek care outside of the VA system once they become due.[7] How does this make sense? Again, extending access to the VA system to veterans' family members would bring substantial savings in Medicare and Medicaid spending while also improving the quality and cost-effectiveness of their health care. Currently, a very few military families have access to the VA, but only for specific treatments when beds are available. In effect, the proposal here involves allowing military families to buy into the VA system while also giving those currently enrolled with Medicare or Medicaid the same option.

Could the VA handle such an increase in its patient load? Certainly not everywhere, and not all at once. Following Hurricane Katrina, VA hospitals in New Orleans and along the Gulf Coast still lie in ruins. Because of the high concentration of retired veterans in central Florida and the absence of any VA hospital there, capacity at VA hospitals and clinics elsewhere in the state is strained to the limit. The same is true in Las Vegas. But remember, in cities and communities across America, dozens of veterans hospitals are slated for closing because they lack sufficient patients to maintain safe volumes of care.

For now, most of these facilities are concentrated in the Midwest, Northeast, and parts of California, where a net out-migration of veterans is occurring.[8] Looking just over the horizon, however, we can see that the same phenomenon will soon spread to many other parts of the country. Today, there are just short of 24 million veterans nationwide. Yet the VA estimates that this will decline to 19.5 million within ten years, and to 14.4 million by 2033.[9] Bear in mind that, even with all the men and women who have served in Afghanistan and Iraq, the number of active duty U.S military personnel as of 2006 was only about a third of what it was in the 1980s, and only a tenth of what it was in 1945.

The drop-off in the numbers of very old veterans, who tend to place the most demand on veterans hospitals, will be particularly sharp over the next twenty years. The number of veterans eighty-five and over, for example, is expected to decline from 253,385 in 2006 to 162,032 in 2026. After that, the number of very old veterans will begin to rise again, as Vietnam vets age into their eighties and beyond. But through at least 2033 there will never again be as many veterans 85 and over as there are today—a trend that is the exact opposite of the aging affecting the U.S. population as a whole.[10]

So why are we making it increasingly harder for veterans to get access to the veterans health care system? Why are we closing VA hospitals instead of opening them up to more veterans and their dependents? In May 2004, the VHA announced it was closing hospitals in Pittsburgh, Pennsylvania, Gulfport, Mississippi, and Brecksville, Ohio.[11] Even after the closures, the VA will still have more than 4 million square feet of real estate it can't find any use for given current eligibility limits. As of this writing, seventeen more VA hospitals are "under review" for closure.

Here is a concrete example. The VA is currently considering closing or consolidating two major medical centers in New York City, one on the east side of midtown Manhattan and the other in the Bay Ridge section of Brooklyn. Together these two facilities employ 360 doctors, who, unlike any other doctors in New York City, use a fully integrated electronic medical record system (VistA) that maximizes patient safety and adherence to the protocols of evidence-based medicine. The Manhattan VA

Medical Center operates 171 beds and specializes in acute medicine, surgery, acute psychiatry, and neurology. The Brooklyn VA Medical Center operates 147 beds and specializes in acute medicine, surgery, psychiatry, and residential substance abuse treatment. Both are affiliated with local medical schools and have a combined research budget of $5.7 million. Both were built in the 1950s and are in good repair. Both would offer the city vital "surge capacity" in the event of a terrorist attack or the widely anticipated avian flu pandemic. Local veterans groups and New York politicians are adamant in their support for the hospitals and have so far managed to keep them open.

But there's a problem: how to maintain enough patients to operate both facilities safely. Large flows of veterans have moved from New York to other parts of the country. A large portion of those left behind are passing away, while tightened eligibility rules mean that most veterans of all ages are excluded from these hospitals. Taken together, these factors lead the VA to project that over the next 20 years, the number of local veterans enrolled in the VA health system will decline by 58 percent, which would leave these two hospitals with mostly empty beds.[12]

What to do? Just maybe society would be best served by razing these hospitals and using the highly valuable land on which they stand to build luxury apartments and condominiums, which is the land's most likely alternative use. Or just maybe, from some point of view that escapes me, it makes sense to let the highly effective doctors and nurses who work in these hospitals drift off to other jobs where they won't have the benefit of VistA and where their interests will no longer be aligned with those of their patients. But somehow I think a more imaginative approach is possible.

TEN

Health for Life

If you spend much time in veterans hospitals or clinics, you quickly notice patients bonding with one another. In the lobby, you are bound to see men trading war stories or asking whatever happened to so-and-so. You also see military wives bonding with each other because they know what it is like to have a husband wounded overseas or to raise a family while moving endlessly from one base to another. There is also often an unusual bond felt between patients and their doctors, many of whom are veterans themselves, or who are at least highly sympathetic to the experience of veterans in American society. All these bonds are a strong and important part of the culture of the VA.

For this reason, I've come to believe that it would not be a good idea to allow people who have no connection to the military to have access to VA hospitals, no matter how logical such a proposal might seem at first. In 1992, when George H.W. Bush's VA secretary, Edward J. Derwinski, suggested opening up three underused VA hospitals in Alabama, Virginia, and Montana to nonveteran Medicaid patients, veterans groups revolted and forced his resignation. Entitling all veterans and their family members to VA health care would go a long way toward forestalling a similar revolt in the future, but one must still anticipate strong political resistance to the idea that veterans should share "their" health care system with outsiders.

But this does not preclude taking steps toward giving all Americans access to the VA *model* of care, which, as we've seen, outperforms any other U.S. health care delivery system in quality, cost-effectiveness, and patient satisfaction. Let's start by giving this idea a name and a slogan. Let's call it VistA Health, because the VA's VistA software and the model of care that it makes possible is what would bind the new system together. Its slogan would be, "Health for Life," because its other prime objective would be to offer Americans who want it continuous and integrated lifetime care.

Already I hear the groans. "Socialized medicine." But if by that you mean removing competition from the health care sector and replacing it with political or bureaucratic fiat, that's not what I have in mind. Under this plan, competition increases between health care providers, many of whom will remain securely in the private sector. The main macrolevel change will be that competition shifts from avoiding costs or maximizing reimbursements to providing the highest value to patients.

The process would start with a demonstration project. Although there are many feasible alternatives, the Boston area would be a prime location. For one reason: Massachusetts has just passed landmark health care insurance legislation that is an essential precondition for making the VistA Health idea work.

The legislation requires all of the state's citizens to acquire health insurance, much as drivers everywhere are required to have drivers' insurance. Massachusetts citizens whose employers offer health insurance will have to accept it or else prove they have coverage from other sources. For those whose employers do not offer health insurance, the state will organize a purchasing pool through which they can acquire insurance at much lower rates than are now available to individuals. For low-income citizens not already covered by the state's Medicaid plan, the state will offer subsidized premiums on a sliding scale.

You are bound to hear a lot more soon about the "Massachusetts model" of health care reform wherever you live. It is a well-crafted "grand bargain" between liberals and conservatives. A Democratic legislature passed the legislation and a Republican governor, Mitt Romney, signed it into law. It enjoys support from think tanks and interest groups across the political spectrum, ranging from the Heritage Foundation and the American Medical Association to labor unions and the Urban Institute. Conservatives like the emphasis on individual responsibility; liberals like the universal coverage.

Both groups like that it solves a problem that besets health insurance markets, which is that many people will only buy health insurance when they think or know they are sick. By one estimate, roughly one-third of the uninsured in Massachusetts earn $90,000 or more a year.[1] They are typically young, healthy people who simply decided to "go bare" because they know there is little chance of their having major medical expenses. This phenomenon, known as "adverse selection," is why insurers charge so much more for individual policies than they do for group insurance. If you show up looking for health insurance as an individual, there is an actuarially demonstrable chance that you know your health care expenses will exceed your premiums. For the VistA Health system to work properly, insurance coverage should be mandatory, as it now is in Massachusetts. Otherwise, the system itself will be encumbered by adverse selection as the young and healthy tend to avoid it and the old and the sick gravitate to it.

How would the VistA Health work? Let's take the concrete example of a demonstration project that might begin in Boston. The Boston area has an incredible fifty-six different hospitals. According to the latest available data, 42 percent of them lost money in 2004. Most are operating on very slender margins. Any one of these financially imperiled hospitals might be attracted by this deal: install the VA's VistA health information management software, agree to adhere to the performance measures and protocols of evidence-based medicine used by the VA itself, and you will secure a contract to care for a guaranteed pool of people.

This pool will consist of local people who have chosen to satisfy the state's requirement that they purchase health insurance by getting their coverage from the new VistA Health system. If you treat them well, most of these patients will stay with you for a long time because they are the ones deciding whether to stay in the plan, not their employers.

At the same time, the VistA Health system will address a huge problem that mandated insurance coverage leaves unsolved or threatens to make worse. The Massachusetts model, for example, does little or nothing by itself to contain the cost of health care, nor to improve its quality. Sure, having every citizen insured should lead to more people getting care before their illnesses become extreme. This will help reduce the strain on emergency rooms that comes from uninsured patients. But aside from this and some brave talk about "pay for performance," Massachusetts has done nothing to change, much less improve, the efficiency and effectiveness of how health care is delivered.

This means, for example, that surgeons who currently perform unnecessary heart surgeries (and there are many in Boston!) or doctors who deliver inappropriate care to their diabetic patients will have that many more patients from whom they can collect insurance money. And by continuing to reward providers for treatment as opposed to prevention or cure, the Massachusetts model preserves the backward incentives that pervade American health care outside of the VA. It is not hard to imagine that after a few years, Massachusetts will be facing an explosion of health care cost—unless that is, it can install a system like VistA Health.

The same would be true if any state, or the country as a whole, ever adopted a "single-payer" system, such as by extending Medicare to all. It's not enough just to improve access to health care. By itself, that increases effective demand for health care and drives up costs, thereby rendering even fewer people able to meet the cost of their own care. Solving the problem of the uninsured is vital, but you must at the same time improve the effectiveness of health care itself or else face unsustainable costs for treatments of little or even negative value. Fortunately, there is ample money in the health care sector today to meet the health care needs of every American, and the VA provides a proven model for how to make the most of it.

Ramping Up

Of course, the single greatest reason the VA is the best health care delivery system in the country is that it truly is a system, with facilities in every market offering continuing, integrated, lifetime care. For this reason, one would not expect a single demonstration project to produce results comparable to the VA system. Scale is all-important. People are more likely to stay in the system, and to get better care from it, if it has facilities available wherever they might happen to move, whether in the course of their career or in retirement. As with any network— railroads, telephones, the Internet—the more people have access to it, the more valuable it becomes for all. And as was true of all three of those examples, government investment and intervention are necessary to get the network growing.

So how could a VistA Health system be ramped up quickly? As in Boston, there are hospitals all over the country that are either already shuttered or facing bankruptcy. Let's put ourselves in the shoes of someone responsible for running one of these financially imperiled hospitals. Call it St. Elsewhere.

As the head of St. Elsewhere, you'd like to install an electronic medical record system, improve prevention, and manage chronic illness effectively. It's what all the smart people in medicine say is the right thing to do these days—at least the ones without MBAs. Your businesspeople tell you there is no way of recapturing the necessary investment because the hospital is paid for treating patients rather than keeping or making them well.

Some of the insurance companies and large employers with which you do business want you to install an electronic medical records system, but the talk is not very tempting. Most of the benefits of such a system are lost if it just stands alone in your hospital. There is no way you can force doctors to use the system in their own office, much less integrate it into their practice. The cost of commercial software is extravagant, and all you have to do is read the medical trade press to learn of horrifying example after example of hospitals that have tried and failed to make it work, much less pay for itself.

Still, the status quo isn't acceptable either. When it comes to other technologies, like imaging devices, you're in an arms race with the other hospitals in your market. At the same time, there is ever more pressure from insurers, larger employers, and increasingly patients themselves to hold down price. Many of the old line manufacturing companies in your area will either have to get control of their health care spending or go out of business. For all these reasons, your bottom line is threatened. But now there is a new player in the market—the VistA Health system. We can imagine this player as being aggressive, or comparatively mellow. At its most aggressive, it might say to a hospital such as yours something like this:

> *If you expect to get paid by Medicare or Medicaid, you'll have to join the VistA Health system. This requires installing VistA software and using it to demonstrate that you are meeting certain VA performance standards. For example, if more than 5 percent of the heart attack patients who leave your hospital are not prescribed with aspirin or beta blockers, there's a penalty for that. Similarly, if you offer admitting privileges to doctors who do not themselves use VistA in both the hospital and their own offices, and adhere to the protocols of medicine embedded in it, there's a penalty for this as well.*

Alternatively, we can imagine this player being less aggressive, yet still persuasive. It might say, for example, something like this:

> *I've just created a new health care plan that individuals and small businesses can use to satisfy the new mandate requiring everyone to purchase health insurance. The terms of the plan are that bene-*

ficiaries will receive their care from a network of providers I am currently putting together. It's called the VistA Health network. Large numbers of patients and dollars are involved; before long, we are going to go national. If you want a piece of this action, you are welcome to put in a proposal. But to qualify, you must install VistA software and adopt the VA model of care. To sweeten the deal, I'll pay for the hardware you need, and also for any support you require in installing and servicing VistA, which itself is free.

Whether mellow or aggressive, such a player is going change the world you have always known. If you join VistA Health, lots of doctors and specialists who practice in your hospital are going to scream. Many are phobic about computers; others, especially the specialists, are going to condemn the model of evidence-based medicine practiced by the VA as "cookbook medicine," and rightly see it as a deep threat to their incomes.

Saying no, however, could become awkward too. For example, how do you explain to patients, insurers, and large employers negotiating contracts with your hospital why you are still using paper records when your competitor across town who joined the VistA Health network is thoroughly wired? How do you explain why your VistA competitor can demonstrate its adherence to the protocols of evidence-based medicine, while you have practically no idea what your doctors are up to and no data to show how effective they might be? And finally, and most crucially, how do you explain why the VistA Health network can beat you on price?

As the VistA Health network extends to more locations, you can also expect that it will offer consumers more advantages, emerging from its sheer size, as well. Once the network becomes national in scale, for example, more people will be tempted to join it just so they can know that, wherever they may happen to get sick in the United States, they'll have access to a facility where their complete medical records are available and where there is no exposure to "out of network" charges.

Even if a hospital or HMO ultimately decided not to join the VistA Health network, being in competition with it would be a spur to improving its own quality. In much the same way as the existence of the U.S. Postal Service forces FedEx and UPS to be far more efficient companies than they would otherwise be, the existence of the VistA Health network pressures other health care providers to match or exceed its performance. If the only way they could do this was by reorganizing into large, integrated systems like Kaiser Permanente, so much the better. Despite the negative press that is a consequence of their sheer size, the only health care providers in the United States that can begin to match the VA's quality performance are big systems like Kaiser.

The same point applies in the opposite direction. VistA would not be a monopoly, nor even a near monopoly like the British health care system, and so it would compete for its customers. One can imagine a day coming when the federal government decrees that all Medicaid and Medicare patients receive their care through VistA-affiliated hospitals and clinics, but VistA would still compete with the private sector for customers not using these programs, just as the VA competes with the rest of the U.S. health care system for the business of veterans. Rechanneling, as opposed to replacing, the role of competition in health care is an essential advantage this approach has over simply nationalizing the U.S. health care system.

Who Pays?

Now let's look at VistA Health from the taxpayers' point of view. For the most part, the people who use the system pay for it in the form of premiums and copayments. VistA could of course be financed entirely by taxes, but why bother? Americans hate taxes, especially those that go for services they don't use themselves. Under a system of mandated insurance, such as that adopted by Massachusetts, there would be no free riders. Nor would there be many cross-subsidies between users and nonusers. The system would essentially be financed by the equivalent of user fees, collected directly by VistA, plus some general revenues to reduce premiums for lower-income participants who do not qualify for Medicaid.

Meanwhile, for every Medicare and Medicaid patient the government can lure or force into VistA, there is a cost savings to the taxpayers, especially over time. It costs the VA only about $80 per patient per year to operate its electronic medical records, which, as Jonathan B. Perlin, acting undersecretary for health, notes, is "Roughly the equivalent of not repeating one blood test."[2] The total amount saved by avoiding unnecessary tests and treatments, as well as by better prevention, disease management, and avoidance of medical errors is hard to quantify, but there is no doubt that the VA model of care is unmatched in its cost-effectiveness. Ken Kizer notes that the VA's cost per elderly patient is only about half to two-thirds that of Medicare. Moreover, the VA's cost per patient is essentially unchanged over the last ten years, while the per capita costs everywhere else in the rest of the U.S. health care system gallop ahead year after year. So the VA cost advantage now will grow much larger over time.

An embellishing idea would be to reward people who perform valuable public service, such as police and firefighters, teachers in inner-city schools, or doctors who agree to practice in rural areas with reduced, or even free, premiums for VistA Health coverage. This would be consistent with the spirit of the veterans health care system. It's not an entitlement; it's recognition for those who serve.[3]

Creating a VistA Health network would not require the government to incur huge capital costs. Though VistA Health might choose to build its own hospitals and clinics in certain underserved locations, such as rural areas and inner cities, or to help pay for the upgrading of existing hospitals and clinics to meet its standards, most VistA-affiliated facilities would still be owned and operated by the private interests, charity organizations, and local governments that own and operate them today. VistA's role in these hospitals and clinics would be analogous to that of a franchiser: setting and enforcing standards and achieving economies of scale in technology, purchasing, information management, and marketing.

VistA Health would certainly advertise the virtues it had to offer consumers. Its ads would drive home the point that its model of care has been shown, in study after study, to be the safest and most effective available in America, while also enjoying the highest rates of consumer satisfaction. Done right, such a public service campaign would get ordinary people concerned if their doctor or hospital didn't have a VistA "Health for Life" logo on the door.

Floods, Bugs, and Bombs

The VistA Health system would also help solve another problem, which is how to maintain enough hospital beds in a community to deal with surges of demand, such as from an epidemic of avian flu, major earthquake, hurricane, or terrorist attack. In Washington, D.C., for example, after a long series of hospital closures, there are only 4,346 hospital beds left—a number that will soon drop with the closing of Walter Reed Army Medical Center's main facilities. Yet projections show that even a moderately severe strain of a pandemic flu virus would require some 5,000 people to be hospitalized in the District alone. Even if every patient in Washington's hospitals was discharged to make room for people struck by avian flu— including all the mental patients in St. Elizabeth's, all the frail elderly in Hadley Memorial's long-term acute care facility, and all the veterans in Washington's VA Medical Center—there would still not be enough hospital beds available to care for, or even to quarantine, highly infectious flu patients.

The same is true nationally. Since 1980, the number of hospital beds available per U.S. resident has declined by roughly 40 percent. Today the United States has only about 965,000 staffed hospital beds. Yet Trust for America's Health, a nonprofit group committed to promoting public health, estimates that the emergence of a pandemic flu virus like the one of 1918 would require hospitalization of 2.3 million people in this country.

There are many sound reasons why the number of hospital beds has been declining. New technology allows for much greater use of outpatient facilities. Galloping medical inflation demands more cost-effective care. But the result is a health care system that will be overwhelmed by a pandemic, major terrorism attack, or natural disaster.

So what to do? As we saw in Chapter 8, simply adding more hospital beds to the current system would be a very bad idea. Hospital beds create their own demand, at least when they are controlled by profit-maximizing doctors and hospitals. But Roemer's law would not apply to a health care system modeled on the VA. The VA has no incentive to fill empty beds just because they are empty. That just brings more expense. The same would be true of VistA-affiliated hospitals, which would receive a fixed sum for treating a fixed population.

Having VistA Health system maintain enough capacity to deal with emergency surge demand would require public subsidies, but this would be more than appropriate. Literally every American, including those who never used VistA, would stand to benefit from a health care system built to handle such increasing risks as a flu pandemic, another Katrina, a major earthquake, or a terrorist attack. As was revealed in New Orleans after Hurricane Katrina, the electronic medical records maintained by VistA software are particularly valuable when large populations become displaced.

Governance

There is legitimate reason to worry that politicians and special interests would become too involved in setting VistA Health's policies. That has certainly been a problem for the VA over the years. Ken Kizer's brilliant leadership at the VA came to an end, for example, after Senator John Kerry objected to his plan to consolidate VA hospitals in Boston and put a hold on Kizer's renomination.[4] The VA has become the best-integrated health care system despite congressional oversight, not because of it.

Unless VistA Health is given some degree of insulation from the political process, it is easy to imagine that medical device makers, for example, might succeed in getting Congress to order VistA, or VistA-affiliated providers, to purchases devices they don't need. Similarly, drug companies could campaign to have their particular pills included in VistA's formulary, and various medical specialists could lobby to have VistA adopt procedures of dubious value into its protocols of care.

For all these reasons, I recommend making VistA Health into an independent agency whose policies would be set by an independent board of outsiders. One model could be the National Academy of Sciences' Institute of Medicine, which, though chartered by Congress, is completely independent, even for its funding. A similar institute could be chartered by Congress to take on the role of establishing protocols of evidence-based medicine for VistA Health, in cooperation with the VA and the Agency for Health Care Policy and Research. One ancillary but important benefit would be to reduce medical malpractice suits. Doctors who followed protocols established by such an independent and, one would hope prestigious, institute would be in a strong position against a plaintiff who claimed to have been given inappropriate care or denied necessary treatments and tests.

The Docs' Point of View

This brings us to how doctors themselves might feel about VistA Health. Many, particularly older, doctors and those primarily driven by the profit motive, would have no interest in working in a VistA-affiliated hospital, clinic, or group practice. Some would have trouble adapting to computers. Others, such as back surgeons, for example, might find that their particular specialties were given little or no place in VistA protocols due to a lack of any evidence that they work, or work as well as some other procedure. For specialists who routinely engage in unnecessary surgery and testing, working in a VistA-affiliated hospital could mean serious loss of income.

But many other doctors—and these are the ones we want to keep in the profession—would be thrilled to be part of a health care delivery system that is truly driven by science, that puts the interests of patients first, that is up-to-date in its use of information technology, requires no interaction with insurance companies, and emphasizes prevention and wellness. Most VA doctors today cannot imagine how they ever got along without electronic medical records. Most love that they don't have to deal with insurance company paper work or worry about paying for malpractice insurance. Most also take pride in being part of a system in which evidence, not profits, determines standards of care.

Many doctors are also attracted to the VA because of its affiliation with medical schools and the chance this gives them to engage in teaching and research. This is an opportunity VistA-affiliated hospitals and clinics could offer to doctors as well. In many parts of the country, where the population of veterans is declining rapidly and VA hospitals are downsizing or threatened with closure, medical schools will need to find new places outside the VA in which to train interns and residents. In places like Boston, where there is both a high concentration of medical schools and a very rapidly shrinking population of veterans, this need will soon become particularly acute. VistA-affiliated hospitals and clinics could save the day for many medical schools that currently depend on the VA to provide a training ground for their students. At the same time, partnering with medical schools would help VistA-affiliated hospitals and clinics to attract high-quality doctors, including many who may wind up getting laid off by the VA in the future as the number of veterans continues to fall.

One open question is whether VistA-affiliated hospitals and clinics should be required to keep their doctors on staff, as the VA does. A staff model certainly reduces incentives for doctors to engage in overtreatment. It also tends to attract doctors who care more about practicing good medicine than maximizing their income. Still, there seems to be no reason why VistA-affiliated hospitals and clinic couldn't contract with private group practices, for example, that agree to install VistA software and follow its protocols of care in exchange for a fixed fee per patient.

The data generated by VistA software would quickly reveal any patterns of over- or undertreatment. VistA software meanwhile can also track how long patients have to wait for an appointment, which means that a doctor who tried to put off seeing patients would be quickly detected, as would those who showed any substantial deviation from the norm in their patterns of care. To sweeten the deal, VistA Health might offer to pay the malpractice premiums of doctors who contract with the system and adhere to its performance standards.

So putting all or even most VistA Health doctors on salary is probably unnecessary. Another consideration is that, especially in small towns and rural areas, there may not be quite enough VistA patients available to justify a staff of VistA Health doctors. If so, the system could contract with private doctors, as the VA itself does in areas where it lacks facilities. These doctors would simply add VistA patients to their exiting caseload after installing VistA software and agreeing to adhere to VistA protocols of care. This could well result in giving even patients who aren't part of VistA Health the benefits of electronic medical records and all the other valuable features of VistA software.

What's in It for You?

Many readers may wonder how VistA Health would offer them any better deal than a large HMO. A key distinction is that VistA Health would have much longer-term relationships with most of its patients than does a typical HMO. From this would flow many benefits, both to individuals and to society.

Those who choose VistA Health will do so because they think it is best for them, not because they were assigned to the system by their employer. They'll have a large range of doctors from whom to choose, particularly if VistA Health adopts the strategy of contracting with private group practices who meet its performance standards. And people won't have to keep changing doctors just because they change employers or move to a new location. As a result, you will be far less likely to argue over what constitutes a preexisting condition, or worry about lost medical records, or haggle with insurance companies or hospitals over who's responsible for paying the bills.

Most importantly, joining VistA would insure you safer, more integrated, more scientifically driven and cost-effective care. Being able to count on a long-term relationship with most of its patients, the VistA system will have institutional incentives to invest in prevention, wellness, and quality care that are lacking in a typical HMO, let alone fee-for-service medicine. VistA Health will insist that its affiliated providers follow protocols that maximize the health and wellness of the population it covers; otherwise it will be on the hook for all the expensive complications that follow when these protocols are not observed. By adopting the VA model of care, there is also good reason to believe that VistA Health will achieve the VA's very high rates of consumer satisfaction, superior safety record, use of electronic medical records, cost-effective treatment protocols, and other accomplishments for which the VA is lauded by experts today.

You might decide that VistA Health is not for you. In the next chapter, we will deal with the real and perceived threats to privacy that come with an integrated medical information system like VistA software. But as with mass transit, VistA Health would offer you benefits even if you didn't choose to use it.

Just as more people riding commuter trains means fewer cars in your way, more people using VistA Health would mean less crowding in your private doctor's waiting room, for example. More people using VistA Health would also mean more people inoculated against contagious diseases that you might catch, such as the flu.

Because of the demonstrated cost-effectiveness of the VA model, more people using VistA also makes it less likely that runaway medical inflation will cause your employer to go broke or force the government to cut spending on Social Security, the military, education, disaster preparedness, or whatever else it is you care most about in government. It also avoids means-testing and the need to ration care on the basis of age or other obnoxious criteria, such as ability to pay.

Implementing the VistA Health system will empower more Americans to become entrepreneurs or otherwise take risks with their careers and savings by freeing them of the need to hold down a job just to secure affordable group health insurance. VistA, and the competition over quality that it would instill among other providers, would also give the United States a high-quality, equitable health care system, rather than one that is ranked only the thirty-sixth best by the World Health Organization.[5] Implementing VistA also means Americans won't wind up working, as current trend lines suggest they will, from January to December just to pay for health care, but will instead be able to enjoy the benefits of a truly affluent society that leaves time for leisure and family life. And the adoption of VistA Health will make it more likely that our loved ones will be with us to a ripe old age, and we with them.

Yes, the health care crisis is solvable. We need only to overcome our ideological preconceptions and personal biases and commit ourselves to the all-American solution the VA model of care provides.

Epilogue

Starting on January 15, 2006, the City of New York began requiring local clinical laboratories to report the results of blood sugar tests performed on individual citizens to the city's health department. The department plans to use the information to improve surveillance for diabetes, which now afflicts an estimated one out of eight New Yorkers, and to "target interventions." Specifically, if you live in New York and have trouble resisting sweets or exercising regularly, your doctor may well soon receive a call from the health department suggesting the need to persuade you to change your lifestyle.

What makes this development so extraordinary in the annals of American public health is that diabetes is not a disease you can catch from, or give to, anyone else. To be sure, American governments have a long history of imposing quarantines and otherwise restricting the liberties of people suspected of carrying contagious disease. Early in the last century, for example, the very same New York City Heath Department famously exiled Mary Mallon (a.k.a. "Typhoid Mary"), along with many other infectious patients, to a tiny island "colony" in the East River.

Existing policies requiring the reporting of sexually transmitted diseases to public health authorities similarly derive justification from the threat of contagion. Even recently enacted smoking bans in New York City and elsewhere only passed after the public accepted findings that "secondhand" smoke poses a serious health threat to others.

But diabetes, though now a fearsome epidemic, is not communicable; nor do the behaviors that lead to or exacerbate the disease (primarily lack of exercise and improper diet) put others at risk of illness. It cannot even be said of diabetics, as is often said of illegal drug users, that their habits foster a life of crime or fund crime syndicates and terrorist networks. So how does it become a matter of public interest that the governments surveil the medical records of individual citizens for telltale signs of high blood sugar, much less "target interventions"? Isn't this the ultimate example of the "nanny state" run amok?

Many readers may have similar fears about the implications of government-controlled electronic medical records and the VA model of health care that these records enable. Many people like the fact that they can consult a doctor without his or her necessarily knowing that they once checked themselves into a psychiatric clinic, or sought treatment for alcoholism or drug abuse, or once had an abortion or venereal disease. Many people also don't want their doctor, let alone an agency of the government, haranguing them about their lifestyle—whether it be smoking, lack of exercise, eating sweets or fats, or whatever—any more than we want our auto mechanics telling us how to drive. Still others fear that their electronic medical records will fall into the wrong hands, thereby subjecting them to blackmail, identity theft, or discrimination by employers and insurance companies.

These are all understandable fears. Some can be allayed by

technology. VistA is constructed so that researchers who mine the data contained in medical records cannot know the identity of whose records they are. Moreover, stealing electronic medical records without detection is often more difficult than stealing paper records. A paper record, for example, shows no sign if it has been photocopied, but VistA keeps a log of everyone who accesses the system and what they do within it.

Yet no one should pretend that a system like VistA does not pose threats to privacy. In 2006, the VA endured justified criticism when a laptop containing individual medical records was stolen from an employee's home.

The question is, are these threats sufficient to negate all the proven advantages VistA brings to the practice of medicine?

A hard truth is emerging in our time that should caution against snap judgments about the sanctity of medical privacy above all other values and goals in health care. Certainly we should continue to expect that our health care records, both paper and electronic, be protected against theft and unauthorized access, and to demand that institutions that are sloppy about their responsibility to protect our records be punished. But maintaining medical privacy in any broader sense is becoming increasingly expensive, both to individuals and to the public. The emerging question is whether medical privacy is simply a basic human right, or something more akin to a privilege for which those who want it should pay rather than shifting the cost onto others.

The primary reason for the increasing cost of medical privacy is the increasing prevalence of chronic diseases like diabetes. Such diseases, which have now become the leading causes of illness and death in advanced societies, typically cannot be prevented, cured, nor even much ameliorated, except by changes in diet and lifestyle that most of us, including myself, are disinclined, perhaps even genetically, to make. The Centers for Disease Control and Prevention attribute nearly half of all deaths in the United States to lifestyle causes, including alcohol consumption (3.5 percent of all deaths) obesity and poor nutrition (16.5 percent), and smoking (18 percent).[1]

The medical treatment of chronic diseases also typically requires highly coordinated and continuous care. It usually involves an array of specialists engaged in care ranging from surgery to intensive patient education, physical therapy, attempted behavioral modification, and, especially in the case of diabetes, constant monitoring. The coordination of such treatment requires sharing of patient information among a broad range of medical professionals, both at any given time and over time. Today, one in seven hospital admissions occurs because care providers do not have access to previous medical records. One out of five lab tests are done for the same reason.[2]

Moreover, advancing our understanding of how best to cure and manage such diseases requires assembling vast amounts of medical data about populations as a whole. There can be no "evidence-based" medicine without collecting evidence about what actually works for most people, most of the time. Lack of free-flowing information in the health care system drives up the cost of health insurance and contributes to the problem of the uninsured. For the population as a whole, it impedes the safe and effective practice of medicine, retards the development of medical protocols based on science, and in all these ways and more reduces productivity and life expectancy.

These are among the big reasons why a broad consensus has emerged, ranging from Hillary Clinton to Newt Gingrich, behind the idea that every American should have a lifelong electronic medical record. But the tradeoff to any increase in the flow of medical information is of course a threat to individual privacy. Deciding in what circumstances the tradeoffs are worth it is the new threshold issue in American health care. Medical privacy is not simply a question of individual right, even for individuals whose medical problems might at first seem purely their own concern.

The creation of a VistA Health system would remove, or at least seriously diminish, one major concern people have about their medical privacy. Enrollment in the system would be open to all, regardless of preexisting conditions. No one would ever again face the prospect of being unable to get health insurance, or to get it at a reasonable price, just because they once tested positive for AIDS or had a cancer tumor detected.

At the same time, however, VistA Health would probably take much more interest in your personal behavior than do the doctors you currently see. Following the VA's clinical guidelines, VA doctors routinely grill their patients about their smoking habits, for example. A survey of VA patients who smoke found that two-thirds had been counseled to quit by their doctor at least once within the last year.[3] Because of its long-term relationship with its patients, the VA has a strong institutional interest in deterring even its youngest patients from unhealthy habits. The VA estimates that smoking, for example, accounts for up to 24 percent of its total health care costs—an expense that is driven up in large measure by the fact that the VA's smokers typically don't move on to other health care plans before they begin experiencing smoking-related illnesses. Accordingly, the VA not only includes counseling against smoking in its clinical guidelines but charges no co-payments for smoking cessation programs, associated drugs, or nicotine patches, the dollar cost of which, for most "civilian" smokers, matches or exceeds that of smoking itself.[4] The VistA Health system, facing the same institutional incentives to promote wellness, would show the same concern, or—"nosiness" if that's how you regard it—about your lifestyle and long-term health.

Could such nosiness eventually be taken so far that it became a serious affront to personal liberty? Sure it could. In my view, the war on drugs is an egregious example of government excess committed in the name of preserving the population's health. But the point remains that medical privacy, far from being free, is getting more expensive all the time, due mostly to the changing nature of disease, which is more and more the result of behavioral and environmental factors. The true libertarian therefore asks, why should I pay for your privacy?

Enacting VistA Health does not mean that every American has to have a lifetime, electronic health record or be treated by a system that has institutional incentives to promote wellness. Nor does it mean that individuals would have to give up their current doctor or forfeit the ability to pick out a new doctor in the future. Those who object to VistA's model of care on whatever grounds would still have the option of going to other sources.

They might thereby find themselves subjected to unnecessary surgeries, high risk of medical errors, and neglect of prevention, as well as being enabled in their addictions and bad habits. Or they might even have the rare but happy experience of finding that one specialist who provides a treatment that, though it's ineffective or harmful to most people, nonetheless works for them.

But choosing to opt out of the VistA Health system would probably cost you a lot of money. Private insurers would likely be glad to sell you a policy that covers care outside the VistA network, including care that is fragmented and unmanaged, and that still clings to nineteenth-century information technology. But the premiums you would have to pay for such a policy would likely be very much higher than those charged by VistA Health.

One reason is the care you would be receiving would be inherently less efficient, more dangerous, less effective, and therefore more costly. Another reason is that your private health care insurer would have to charge you a large "risk premium" to overcome the problem of adverse selection. The underwriters would be forced to consider that you have opted out of lower-cost VistA Health because you are looking for heroic or unproven treatments not offered by VistA—a risk to their capital for which they will have to charge you.

Also, the more medical information you insist remain unknown to the insurance company, such as the results of lab tests, the higher the premium the underwriters will have to charge you to overcome the uncertainty created by your demand for privacy. Any asymmetry of information between insurer and insuree necessarily drives up the cost of insurance. In a coming age of effective genetic testing and other means of better predicting individual susceptibility to disease, the price of medical privacy may well rise so high as to wreck the private health insurance market for all but the super rich or super fit.[5]

This, I believe, is the future of twenty-first-century medicine. One tendency of modern society is for us to become convinced of our individuality. We increasingly come to see ourselves as unique, not only in how our mind works but also our body. At the same time, we come to see ourselves as endowed with a bundle of universal liberties, including the freedom to eat, drink, or smoke whatever, drive wherever, sleep with whomever, and then choose whichever doctors and medical treatments we might want to try to deal with the consequences.

Yet a countervailing tendency heightens our objective dependency on others, however much we may hate to admit it. The percentage of the population suffering with chronic health conditions increases year after year. The percentage of Americans who can pay for their own health care decreases year after year. Progress in medicine continues, but as new drugs and treatment options proliferate, the consumer becomes lost in a sea of competing claims. Can Lexapro really cure generalized anxiety disorder? Does the syndrome really exist, and how could I tell if I had it? How can I tell if arthroscopic knee surgery is right for me, let alone find a surgical team that can perform the operation without giving me a staph infection? Such questions cannot be answered with a Google search.

Reconciling these two tendencies—increased individualism combined with increased objective dependence on others—will be a central theme of American politics for years to come. Neither pure socialized medicine nor pure market-driven medicine offers an acceptable solution. But giving all Americans the option to try out the high-quality, cost-effective "Health for Life" model of care pioneered by the VA will make for a stronger and healthier nation while also preserving our individual right as Americans to make the wrong decision.

Acknowledgments

My deep thanks go to Bernard L. Schwartz, whose generous support of the New America Foundation provided me with the time and intellectual freedom I needed to research and write this book. I am also grateful to the many people who agreed to lend their time and expertise as I set out to report on the VA. I am particularly indebted to Dr. Donald Berwick of the Institute for Health Care Improvement and Dr. Elliot S. Fisher of Dartmouth Medical School for teaching me new ways to look at health care. Dr. Kenneth Dickie, formerly of the VA, not only sat with me for an extensive interview, but also provided me with invaluable access to his personal archive of material related to the VA's early and tumultuous experiments with digitalized health care. Dr. Scott Shreeve, founder of Medsphere—a company committed to bringing the VA model of care to the private sector—was also very generous with his time, insights, and archives.

Thanks go as well to Paul Glastris, editor-in-chief of the *Washington Monthly*, for his help in formulating many of the ideas in this book, and for having the courage publish my 2005 cover story on the VA. Shannon Brownlee, Len Nichols, and Sherle Schwenninger of the New America Foundation, as well as Peter Richardson and Scott Jordan of PolipointPress, were also very helpful in their comments. Brian Beutler provided invaluable research help and Jeannette Warren provided essential editing of the early manuscripts. I am also very grateful to Tim Noah for agreeing to write the foreword, and to my wife, Sandy, for understanding why I needed to write this book.

Notes

Foreword

1. Relman A. The Health of Nations, New Republic On-line, March 7, 2005, http://www.tnr.com/doc.mhtml?i=20050307&s=relman030705&c=2.
2. Krugman P, Wells R. The health care crisis and what to do about it, *New York Review of Books*, Volume 53, Number 5, March 23, 2006. http://www.nybooks.com/articles/18802.
3. Ibid.

Introduction

1. Corrigan J, et al, eds. *To Err Is Human: Building a Safer Health System.* Washington, DC: Institute of Medicine, the National Academies Press; 2000; and editorial, Preventing fatal medical errors, *New York Times*, December 1, 1999, p. 22a.
2. Himmelstein DU, et al. Illness and injury as contributors to bankruptcy. *Health Affairs* (Millwood) 2005;Jan–Jun;Suppl Web Exclusives:W5-63–W5-73. http://content.healthaffairs.org/cgi/content/full/hlthaff.w5.63/DC1.
3. Congressional Budget Office. *Long-Term Budget Outlook.* Washington, DC: U.S. Government Printing Office; 2005. Table, Figure 3-2, http://www.cbo.gov/ftpdocs/69xx/doc6982/12-15-LongTermOutlook.pdf.
4. Cox M, Alm R. *Time Well Spent: The Declining Real Cost of Living in America.* 1997 Annual Report, Federal Reserve Bank of Dallas.
5. Blendon RJ, Benson JM. Americans' views on health policy: a fifty-year historical perspective. *Health Affairs* 2001;20(2):39, Exhibit 5.
6. National Center for Health Statistics. *Health, United States, 2005, with Chartbook on Trends in the Health of Americans.* Hyattsville, MD: NCHS; 2005, Table 27. Life expectancy at birth, at 65 years of age, and at 75 years

of age, according to race and sex: United States, selected years 1900–2002, and National Center for Health Statistics, *National Vital Statistics Reports*, 2003;52(3). www.cdc.gov/nchs.

7. Bunker JP. The role of medical care in contributing to health improvements within societies. *International Journal of Epidemiology* 2001; 30: 1260–1263. http://ije.oxfordjournals.org/cgi/content/full/30/6/1260.

8. Cutler DM, et al. The value of medical spending in the United States, 1960–2000. *New England Journal of Medicine* 2006;355(9):920–927. http://content.nejm.org/cgi/content/full/355/9/920#R11. Numbers are adjusted to present value.

9. Strunk BC, Ginsburg PB. *Aging Plays Limited Role in Health Care Cost Trends*. Center for the Study of Health System Change, Data Bulletin No. 23, September 2002, http://www.hschange.com/CONTENT/473/.

10. For a discussion of the ineffectiveness of heart surgery, see Haldler NM, *The Last Well Person*. Montreal: McGill-Queen's University Press; 2004.

11. For a useful summary of this sad chapter in American medicine, see Welch HG, Mogielnicki J. Presumed benefit: lessons from the American experience with marrow transplantation for breast cancer. *British Medical Journal* 2002;324;1088–1092.

12. Banks J, Marmot M, Oldfield Z, Smith JP. Disease and disadvantage in the United States and in England. *Journal of the American Medical Association* 2006;295:2037–2045.

13. World Health Organization. Core health indicators. http://www3.who.int/whosis/country/compare.cfm?language=english&country=cri&indicator=strPcTotEOHinUSD2002.

14. World Health Organization. Global atlas of the health workforce. http://www.who.int/globalatlas/default.asp.

15. World Health Organization: Core health indicators. http://www3.who.int/whosis/country/compare.cfm?language=english&country=cri&indicator=strPcTotEOHinUSD2002.

One

1. Findlay S. Military medicine. *U.S. News & World Report*, June 15, 1992, p. 72.

2. "Clinton's health-care plan for you: cradle-to-grave slavery," http://www.amatecon.com/etext/dosm/dosm-ch04.html.

3. Bauman RE. *70 Years of Federal Government Health Care: A Timely Look at the U.S. Department of Veterans Affairs*. Cato Policy Analysis No. 207. http://www.cato.org/pubs/pas/pa207es.html.

4. Longman P. *The Return of Thrift: How the Collapse of the Middle Class*

Welfare State Will Reawaken Values in America. New York: Free Press; 1996, chapter 10.

5. Jha AK, Perlin JB, Kizer KW, Dudley RA. Effect of the transformation of the veterans affairs health care system on the quality of care, *New England Journal of Medicine,* Volume 348:2218–2227, Number 22, May 29, 2003. http://content.nejm.org/cgi/content/abstract/348/22/2218.

6. Kerr E, Gerzoff R, Krein S, Selby J, Piette J, et al. A comparison of diabetes care quality in the veterans health care system and commercial managed care. *Annals of Internal Medicine* 2004;141(4):272–281. http://www.ncbi.nlm.nih.gov/entrez/query.fcgi?cmd=Retrieve&db=pubmed&dopt=Abstract&list_uids=15313743.

7. Asch SM, McGlynn EA, Hogan MM, Hayward RA, Shekelle P, Rubenstein L, Keesey J, Adams J, Kerr EA. Comparison of quality of care for patients in the Veterans Health Administration and patients in a national sample. *Annals of Internal Medicine* 2004;141(12): pp. 938–945.

8. Selim AJ, Kazis LE, Rogers W, Qian S, Rothendler JA, Lee A, Ren XS, Haffer SC, Mardon R, Miller D, Spiro A 3rd, Selim BJ, Fincke BG. Risk-adjusted mortality as an indicator of outcomes: comparison of the Medicare Advantage Program with the Veterans' Health Administration. *Medical Care* 2006;44(4):359–365.

9. National Committee for Quality Assurance. *The State of Health Care Quality: 2004.* Washington, DC: National Committee for Quality Assurance; 2004. www.ncqa.org/communications/somc/SOHC2004.PDF. Perlin JB. The Veterans Health Administration: quality, value, accountability, and information as transforming strategies for patient-centered care. *American Journal of Managed Care* November 2004, Table 2. http://www.ajmc.com/Article.cfm?ID=2767.

10. ACSI Scores for U.S. Federal Government, American Customer Satisfaction Index I, December 15, 2005. http://www.theacsi.org/government/govt-05.html.

11. *Performance and Accountability Report, FY 2005,* part II, Department of Veterans Affairs, Table 2–FY 2005 Performance Measures by Program. http://www.va.gov/budget/Report/2005/Table2.pdf#search=%22Veterans%20Health%20Administration%20%20Performance%20and%20Accountability%20Report%20%2F%20FY%202005%20%22.

12. Health IT Strategic Framework, Attachment 2, III. The VA Electronic Health Record, VHA Office of Quality and Performance. http://www.hhs.gov/healthit/attachment_2/iii.html.

13. Leape LL, Berwick DM. Five years after *To Err Is Human:* what have we learned? *Journal of the American Medical Association* 2005; 293: 2384–2390.

14. *Journal of the American Medical Association,* January 17, 2001. Jha

AK, Shlipak MG et al. Racial differences in mortality among men hospitalized in the veterans affairs health care system, *Journal of the American Medical Association,* 2001;285:297–303.

15. Healthcare program serving U.S. vets wins government innovation award: hi-tech VistA program one of two federal initiatives to win $100K grant. Press release, Ash Institute for Democratic Governance and Innovation at Harvard University's Kennedy School of Government. July 10, 2006. http://www.innovations.va.gov/innovations/docs/Harvard NewsRelease.pdf.

16. Robert A. Petzel, Director, Veterans Integrated Service Network 23, Compelled to act: it's called survival, PowerPoint presentation, slide 14, available at http://www.amq.ca/congres2006/pdf/Compelled_to_Act-Robert_Petzel.pdf#search=%22%22veterans%20health%20administration %22%20%22per%20enrollee%22%20%22.

17. *Performance and Accountability Report, FY 2005,* part II, Department of Veterans Affairs, Table 2–FY 2005 Performance Measures by Program. http://www.va.gov/budget/Report/2005/Table2.pdf#search=%22Veterans%20Health%20Administration%20%20Performance%20and%20Ac countability%20Report%20%2F%20FY%202005%20%22

18. Centers for Medicare and Medicaid Studies. National health expenditures aggregate and per capita amounts, percent distribution, and average annual percent growth, by source of funds: selected calendar years 1960–2004. http://www.cms.hhs.gov/NationalHealthExpendData/downloads/tables.pdf.

19. Asch SM, et al. Who is at greatest risk for receiving poor-quality health care? *New England Journal of Medicine* 2006;354:1147–1156. http://content.nejm.org/cgi/citmgr?gca=nejm;354/11/1147.

20. Ibid.

21. Office of the Press Secretary, the White House, April 27, 2004. President Bush touts benefits of health care information technology, Department of Veterans Affairs Medical Center, Baltimore, Maryland. http://www.whitehouse.gov/news/releases/2004/04/20040427-5.html.

Two

1. Russell R. *The Shadow of Blooming Grove: Warren G. Harding in His Times.* Reprint. Norwalk, CT: Easton Press; 1988.

2. Daugherty HM. *The Inside Story of the Warren G. Harding Tragedy.* Whitefish, Mont.: Kessing Publishing; 1960:179.

3. Quoted by Klein R. *Wounded Men, Broken Promises.* New York: Macmillan; 1981:41. *Only Yesterday.* New York: HarperCollins; 1931.

4. Klein, op. cit. p. 42.

5. Quoted by Klein, ibid., p. 42.

6. Department of Veterans Affairs, Office of Facilities Management. History of veterans healthcare. http://www.va.gov/facmgt/historic/ Medical_Care.asp.

7. Ibid.

8. The National Institutes of Health and The Veterans Administration. Advisory Committee on Human Radiation Experiments—Final Report, Chapter 1. http://www.eh.doe.gov/ohre/roadmap/achre/chap1_4.html; George M. Lyon, M.D., Assistant Chief Medical Director for Research and Education, presentation to the Committee on Veterans Medical Problems, National Research Council, 8 December 1952 (Appendix II, Medical Research Programs of the Veterans Administration) (ACHRE No. VA-052595-A). http://www.gwu.edu/~nsarchiv/radiation/dir/mstreet/com meet/meet3/brief3.gfr/tab_i/br3i1c.txt.

9. Shortly before he died in 2001, an interviewer asked Ken Kesey how he first came to experiment with LSD. He answered: "I was connected to the VA hospital. Vic Lovell was working over there as a student of some kind, and when the drug experiment started, they set up a version of the VA hospital in Palo Alto. I went over and applied for a job, and a week or so later had a job. They put me on the same ward with the doctor that'd given me those early pills. He was not doing his experimentation anymore; he had quickly learned that this could be a real problem for the American government. One night, I came back in with my keys and went into his room, into his desk, and took out a lot of stuff. That was the source of most of our—all of our drugs—for a long time. See "Digital Interviews" website: http://www.digitalinterviews.com/digitalinterviews/ views/kesey.shtml.

10. Quoted by Klein, ibid., p. 62.

Three

1. Doctors pull plug on paperless system: California's Cedars-Sinai turns off its computerized physician order entry system after physicians revolt, demonstrating that implementing new technology is easier said than done. *American Medical News* Feb. 17, 2003.

2. Evans Witt, Associated Press, March 20, 1977.

3. Brown SH, et al. VistA-U.S. Department of Veterans Affairs national-scale HIS. *International Journal of Medical Informatics* 2003;69:136–135.

4. Interview June 28, 2006.

5. Timson G. The history of the Hardhats. http://www.hardhats.org/ history/hardhats.html.

6. Ibid.

7. Ibid.

8. Ibid.

9. Brown SH, et al. *International Journal of Medical Informatics* 2003;69:136–135.

10. Computers: new look at VA woes. *U.S. Medicine* November 15, 1981.

11. VA decentralization: scaling problems down. *U.S. Medicine* April 1, 1982, p. 3.

12. Interview by David MacFarlane, July 14, 2005, transcript provided by Scott Shreeve, chief medical officer, cofounder, Medsphere Systems Corporation, Aliso Viejo, CA.

13. Computers: new look at VA woes. *U.S. Medicine* November 15, 1981.

14. Timson G. The history of the Hardhats. http://www.hardhats .org/history/hardhats.html.

15. Cited by Brown SH, et al. op. cit. p. 138.

16. Operating MUMP systems are integrated without hitch. *U.S. Medicine*, August 15, 1982, p. 1.

17. Timson G. The history of the Hardhats. http://www.hardhats .org/history/hardhats.html.

18. Tomich N. Congress urged to fund DHCP. *U.S. Medicine*, May 1987, p. 1.

Four

1. Interview by Spotswood S. Quality, access priorities in VA cancer care. *U.S. Medicine* October, 2005. http://www.usmedicine.com/article .cfm?articleID=1167&issueID=80.

2. Remarks of Jonathan Perlin, Undersecretary for Health Affairs, Department of Veteran Affairs, to Ash Institute of the John F. Kennedy School of Government at Harvard University, July 10, 2006.

3. Spotswood S. VA flu vaccination plan prepares patients. *U.S. Medicine* January 2006, http://www.usmedicine.com/article.cfm?articleID= 1236&issueID=83.

4. Management Brief, Health Services Research & Development Service, No. 6, December, 2002. http://www.research.va.gov/resources/ pubs/docs/hsr_brief_no6.pdf.

5. Khuri SF, et al. The Department of Veterans Affairs' NSQIP: the first national, validated, outcome-based, risk-adjusted, and peer-controlled program for the measurement and enhancement of the quality of surgical

care. National VA Surgical Quality Improvement Program. *Annals of Surgery* 1998;228(4):491–507.

6. Interviewed by Spangler D. VA electronic Rx records aid Katrina relief response. *U.S. Medicine*, November 2005. http://www.usmedicine .com/article.cfm?articleID=1202&issueID=81.

Five

1. More than veterans need. *St. Petersburg Times* (Florida), January 16, 1996, editorials, p. 10A.

2. Audit of Veterans Health Administration Resource Allocation Issues: Physician Staffing Levels; 5R8-A19-113, Department of Veteran's Affairs, Office of Inspector General, September 29, 1995. http://www.va .gov/oig/52/reports/1995/5R8-A19-113%20—%20psrptasc.htm.

Kilborn PT. Veterans expand hospital system in face of cuts. *New York Times*, January 14, 1996, sec. 1, p. 1, col. 3; National Desk.

3. Ibid.

4. Part Three: The VHA Transformation As Viewed by Dr. Kenneth W. Kizer, Former Undersecretary for Health, U.S. Department of Veterans Affairs. http://www.businessofgovernment.org/pdfs/Young_Report.pdf.

5. Vision for change: a plan to restructure the Veterans Health Administration, March 17, 1995. http://www.va.gov/vhareorg/vision/2chap1 .doc.

6. http://www.manhattan-institute.org/html/mpr_02.htm.

7. Blumenthal D, Herdman R, eds., VA Pharmacy Formulary Analysis Committee, Division of Health Care Services. Description and analysis of the VA National Formulary 2000, executive summary at: http://darwin .nap.edu/execsumm_pdf/9879.pdf.

8. Interviewed by Smith S. Recasting the lowly formulary. *Minnesota Medicine*, April 2006, v. 89. http://www.mmaonline.net/publications/ MNMed2006/April/quality-smith.htm.

Six

1. Corrigan J, et al, eds. *To Err Is Human: Building a Safer Health System.* Washington, DC: Institute of Medicine, the National Academies Press; 2000. http://darwin.nap.edu/books/0309068371/html/R1.html.

2. Centers for Disease Control and Prevention. Monitoring hospital-acquired infections to promote patient safety—United States, 1990–1999. *Morbidity and Mortality Weekly Report* 2000;49:149–153.

3. *Preventing Medication Errors.* Washington, DC: Institute of Medi-

cine, National Academies Press; 2007. http://darwin.nap.edu/books/0309101476/html.

4. The First National Report Card on Quality of Health Care in America. www.rand.org/publications/RB/RB9053-1/RB9053-1.pdf, page 4.

5. Office of the Medical Inspector, VHA. VA Patient Safety Event Registry: first nineteen months of reported cases summary and analysis, June 1997 through December 1998. Pear R. Report outlines medical errors in VA hospitals. *New York Times*, December 19, 1999, sec. 1, p. 1, col. 6.

6. Wiebe C. Patient safety concerns could spur bar code adoption. *Medscape Money & Medicine* 2002;3(2). http://www.medscape.com/viewarticle/440200.

7. Wood D. RN's visionary bar code innovation helps reduce medication errors. NurseZone.com, April 30, 2004. http://www.bridgemedical.com/04_30_04_a.shtml.

8. Johnson CL, Carlson RA, Tucker CL, Willette C. Using BCMA software to improve patient safety in Veterans Administration medical centers. *Journal of Healthcare Information Management* 16(1). http://www.himss.org/content/files/ambulatorydocs/BCMASoftwareTo ImprovePatientSafety.pdf.

9. Leape LL, Berwick DM. Five years after *To Err Is Human: What Have We Learned? Journal of the American Medical Association* 2005;293:2384–2390.

Seven

1. Kleinke JD. Dot-gov: market failure and the creation of a national health information technology system. *Health Affairs* 2005;24(5):1246–1262.

2. Casalino L. Markets and medicine: barriers to creating a "business case for quality." *Perspectives in Biology and Medicine* 2002;46(1):38–51.

3. Urbina I. In the treatment of diabetes, success often does not pay. *New York Times*, January 11, 2006, p. 1. http://www.nytimes.com/2006/01/11/nyregion/nyregionspecial5/11diabetes.html?pagewanted=1&ei=5070&en=6c6db1d60e88d20b&ex=1148097600.

4. Snyderman R, Williams RW. The new prevention. *Modern Healthcare* 2003;33:19. Congestive heart failure: comprehensive heart failure teams reduce health care costs. *Health & Medicine Week* 2000. http://www.newsrx.com/newsletters/Health-and-Medicine-Week/2004-04-01/20000401333235W.html.

5. *Improving Health Care: A Dose of Competition.* Report by the Federal Trade Commission and the Department of Justice, July 2004, p. 24. http://www.ftc.gov/reports/healthcare/040723healthcarerpt.pdf.

6. Pursuing perfection in Whatcom County (WWPP). Home page: http://www.wwpp.org:8080/wwppDiscuss/.

7. Jack Homer, et al. Models for collaboration: how system dynamics helped a community organize cost-effective care for chronic illness. See chart, p. 30. http://www.wwpp.org/static/gems/wwppDiscuss/sdp.pdf #search=%22Models%20for%20Collaboration%3A%20How%20System %20Dynamics%20Helped%20%22.

8. Kolata G. Health plan that cuts costs raises doctors' ire. *New York Times,* May 18, 2006. www.nytimes.com/pages/national/index.html.

9. Anderson GF, et al. Health care spending and use of information technology in OECD countries. *Health Affairs* 2006;25(3):819–831.

10. Brown SH, et al. *International Journal of Medical Informatics* 2003; 69:135–156, appendix B: VistA adopters outside of VA. http://www1.va .gov/cprsdemo/docs/VistA_Int_Jrnl_Article.pdf.

11. Rossi S. International expertise sought on e-health standards. *Computerworld: The Voice of IT Management.* (Australia). http://www .computerworld.com.au/index.php/id;358080262;fp;2;fpid;1.

12. Aldrich M. *Safety First: Technology, Labor, and Business in the Building of American Work Safety, 1870–1939.* Studies in Industry and Society. Baltimore: Johns Hopkins University Press; 1997.

13. Kaiser/HRET Survey of Employer Sponsored Health Benefits, 2005. Kaiseredu.org. http://www.kaiseredu.org/tutorials/uninsured/ uninsured_update.html, slide 9.

14. Porter M, Olmsted Teisberg E. *Redefining Health Care: Creating Value-Based Competition on Results.* Cambridge, MA: Harvard Business School; 2006.

15. Greenhouse S, Leonhardt D. Real wages fail to match a rise in productivity. *New York Times,* August 28, 2006. http://www.nytimes.com/ 2006/08/28/business/28wages.html?ex=1165986000&en=c9613e1156ddf ce5&ei=5070.

16. Payne JW. Your kind of doctor. *Washington Post,* January 31, 2006. http://www.washingtonpost.com/wp-dyn/content/article/2006/01/ 30/AR2006013001238.html.

17. Press release, Destiny Health, Opinion Research Corporation. Study reveals Americans resist doing healthcare homework; making more information available may not solve cost crisis. http://home.businesswire.com/ portal/site/google/index.jsp?ndmViewId=news_view&newsId=20060814 005734&newsLang=en.

18. Baker DW, Einstadter D, Thomas, C, et al. The effect of publicly reporting hospital performance on market share and risk-adjusted mortality at high-mortality hospitals. *Medical Care* 2003;41(6):729–740. http:// www.ahrq.gov/research/oct03/1003RA3.htm.

Eight

1. Williams M. The doctor factor. *Washington Post*, December 31, 2003, p. A19. http://www.washingtonpost.com/wp-dyn/articles/A43185-2003 Dec30.html.

2. Wennberg JE, Gittelsohn AM. Variations in medical care among small areas. *Science*, December 14, 1973, pp. 1102–1108.

3. Fitzhugh M. Wrestling with variation: an interview with Jack Wennberg. *Health Affairs*, web exclusive. http://content.healthaffairs.org/cgi/reprint/hlthaff.var.73v1.

4. Fisher ES, Wennberg DE, Stukel TA, Gottlieb DJ, Lucas FL, Pinder EL. The implications of regional variations in Medicare spending, II: Health outcomes and satisfaction with care. *Annals of Internal Medicine* 2003;138:288–298.

5. Fisher ES, Wennberg DE, Stukel TA, Gottlieb DJ, Lucas FL, Pinder EL. The implications of regional variations in Medicare spending, I: The content, quality, and accessibility of care. *Annals of Internal Medicine* 2003; 138:273–287.

6. Gibbs N, Bower A. Q: What scares doctors? A: Being the patient. *Time*, May 1, 2006 (cover).

7. Roemer MI. Bed supply and hospital utilization: a natural experiment. *Hospitals* 1961;35:36–42.

8. Heart procedure is off the charts in an Ohio City. *New York Times*, August 18, 2006, Business Desk. http://www.nytimes.com/2006/08/18/business/18stent.html?ex=1156996800&en=9a672c108ed8640c&ei=5070.

9. Gagnet K. Lourdes to pay $3.8M: hospital admits no fault in Patel-related matter. *Daily Advertiser* (Lafayette, La.), August 18, 2006. www.theadvertiser.com/apps/pbcs.dll/article?AID=/20060818/NEWS01/608180316/1002.

10. Anderson-Cloud RL. Merging a divided system: the need to integrate care for individuals participating in both the Medicare and Medicaid Programs. *Age in Action*, Summer 1999. http://www.vcu.edu/vcoa/ageaction/agesu99.htm.

11. Does managed care need to be replaced? Presentation to the Graduate School of Management, University of California, Irvine, October 2, 2001. http://www.medscape.com/viewarticle/408185.

12. Enthoven A. Post-mortem on managed care. *CommonWealth*, Fall 2005. (Review of Gregoire Coombs J. *The Rise and Fall of HMOs: An American Health Care Revolution*. Madison: University of Wisconsin Press. http://www.massinc.org/index.php?id=481&pub_id=1697&bypass=1.

13. Gruenberg EM. The failures of success. Paper presented as the Rema Lapouse lecture at the Annual Meeting of the American Public Health Association, Miami, Florida, October 19, 1976, reprinted in the *Mil-*

bank Memorial Fund Quarterly, 1977;55(1):3–24. http://www.milbank
.org/quarterly/830424gruenberg.pdf.

14. White K. The ecology of medical care: origins and implications for
population-based healthcare. *Health Services Research* 1997;32(1):11–21.

Nine

1. Text of Clinton Statement on Veterans-Related Bills, WASHING-
TON, U.S. Newswire Oct. 9, 1996.

"The second bill—H.R. 3118, the Veterans' Health Care Eligibility
Reform Act of 1996—includes many elements of the proposal that the
National Performance Review, led by Vice President Gore, recommended
to establish a modern, integrated health care system that will improve
access to, and care for, the Nation's veterans. The bill, for instance, authorizes the Department of Veterans Affairs to furnish comprehensive medical
services to all veterans, expanding the array of services that it now provides. Eligibility reform has been a high priority of veterans for many
years, and I am pleased that we finally could enact it." http://veterans
.house.gov/hearings/schedule106/july99/7-15/gao.htm.

2. www.va.gov/healtheligibility/Resource/pubs/fs16-3.pdf/.

3. DOCKET NO. 97-12 065, http://www.va.gov/vetapp98/files2/
9815037.txt.

4. Statement of Ron Garvin, Acting Chairman of the Board of Veterans
Appeals, May 5, 2005. http://veterans.house.gov/hearings/schedule109/
may05/5-5-05m/5-5-05eo.pdf.

5. "H.R. 515, Assured Funding for Veterans Health Care Act of 2005.
As introduced on February 2, 2005,"Congressional Budget Office, July
25, 2005. http://www.cbo.gov/showdoc.cfm?index=6574&sequence=0.

6. Himmelstein DU, Woolhandler S. America's neglected veterans: 1.7
million who served have no health coverage. Report of the Harvard/
Cambridge Hospital Study Group on Veterans' Health Insurance. http://
www.pnhp.org/Veterans/veteran.pdf.

7. S. 1182, Veterans Health Care Act of 2005, Congressional Budget
Office, October 14, 2005. http://www.cbo.gov/showdoc.cfm?index
=6783&sequence=0.

8. California's veterans population is declining by 14,500 persons per
year; New York's by 10,600. http://www.va.gov/vetdata/demographics/
Vetpop2004/data/5l.xls.

9. VetPop2004 1.0 Table 5L: Veterans 2000–2033 by Race/Ethnicity,
Gender, Period, Age. http://www.va.gov/vetdata/Demographics/
Vetpop2004/vp2004v1.htm.

10. Ibid.

11. Lee C. VA to close some hospitals, build others. *Washington Post,* May 8, 2004, A Section; A04.

12. Capital Asset Realignment for Enhanced Services (CARES) stage I summary report—Brooklyn–Manhattan VAMCS. Veterans Health Administration, August 2005. http://www.va.gov/CARES/Documents/Brooklyn_2005_09_19_SummaryReport.pdf.

Ten

1. Interview with Michael Porter. Can this man fix our healthcare system? *Across the Board,* July/August 2006. http://www.conference-board.org/articles/atb_article.cfm?id=355.

2. Quoted by Gaul GM. Revamped veterans' health care now a model. *Washington Post,* August 22, 2005, p. A01.

3. Longman P. Best care, anywhere. *Washington Monthly,* January/February 2005, pp. 39–48.

4. Press release, office of Senator Kerry. Dr. Kenneth Kizer will not seek renomination as VA under secretary for healthcare, June 29, 1999.

5. The World Health Report 2000—health systems: improving performance. World Health Organization, Geneva, Switzerland. http://www.who.int/whr/2000/en/whr00_en.pdf.

Epilogue

1. Mokdad AH, Marks JS, Stroup DF, Gerberding JL. Actual causes of death in the United States, 2000. *Journal of the American Medical Association* 2004;291:1238–1245; and Actual causes of death in the United States, 2000—correction. *Journal of the American Medical Association* 2005;293:298.

2. Yasnoff WA. *National Health Information Infrastructure: Key to the Future of Health Care.* U.S. Dept. of Health and Human Services; 2002.

3. Sherman SE, et al. Smokers' interest in quitting and services received: using practice information to plan quality improvement and policy for smoking cessation. *American Journal of Medical Quality* 2005;20(1). http://ajm.sagepub.com/cgi/reprint/20/1/33.

4. *Federal Register,* vol. 70, no. 83 / Monday, May 2, 2005 / Rules and Regulations, 38 CFR Part 17 RIN 2900–AM11, Elimination of copayment for smoking cessation counseling.

5. For a fuller treatment of how medical privacy drives up the cost of private health insurance, see Longman P, Brownlee S. The genetic surprise. *Wilson Quarterly,* October 1, 2000. http://www.newamerica.net/index.cfm?pg=article&DocID=244.

Index

About the Author

Phillip Longman, a senior fellow at the New America Foundation, is the author of numerous articles and books on health care, demographics, and public policy. His most recent book, *The Empty Cradle*, was published by Basic Books in March 2004. The book examines how the rapid yet uneven fall in birth rates around the globe is affecting the evolution of culture and politics. Mr. Longman is also the author of *Born to Pay: The New Politics of Aging in America* (1987) and *The Return of Thrift: How the Collapse of the Middle Class Welfare State Will Reawaken Values in America* (1996).

Mr. Longman's work has appeared in such publications as the *Atlantic, Financial Times, Foreign Affairs, Foreign Policy,* the *Harvard Business Review,* the *New Republic,* the *New York Times Magazine,* the *Wall Street Journal, Washington Monthly, Washington Post, and the Wilson Quarterly.* He is a frequent public speaker, including addresses to the National War College, the Department of Health and Human Services, PopTech, and *Fortune* magazine's annual "Brainstorm" conference. He is also frequently interviewed by both foreign and domestic media, including National Public Radio, the British Broadcasting Corporation, the Canadian Broadcasting Corporation, *Der*

Spiegel, and many others. Formerly a senior writer and deputy assistant managing editor at *U.S. News & World Report*, he has won numerous awards for his business and financial writing, including UCLA's Gerald Loeb Award, and the top prize for investigative journalism from Investigative Reporters and Editors.

Other Books from PoliPointPress

The Blue Pages:
A Directory of Companies Rated by Their Politics and Practices
Helps consumers match their buying decisions with their political
values by listing the political contributions and business practices
of over 1,000 companies.
$9.95, PAPERBACK.

JOE CONASON, *The Raw Deal: How the Bush Republicans Plan to
Destroy Social Security and the Legacy of the New Deal*
Reveals the well-financed and determined effort to undo the Social
Security Act and other New Deal programs.
$11.00, PAPERBACK.

WILLIAM RIVERS PITT, *House of Ill Repute: Reflections on
War, Lies, and America's Ravaged Reputation*
Skewers the Bush Administration for its reckless invasions,
warrantless wiretaps, lethally incompetent response to Hurricane
Katrina, and other scandals and blunders.
$16.00, PAPERBACK.

CURTIS WHITE, *The Spirit of Disobedience: Resisting the Charms
of Fake Politics, Mindless Consumption, and the Culture of Total Work*
Debunks the notion that liberalism has no need for spirituality and
describes a "middle way" through our red state/blue state political
impasse. Includes three powerful interviews with John DeGraaf,
James Howard Kunstler, and Michael Ableman.
$24.00, HARDCOVER.

JEFF COHEN, *Cable News Confidential: My Misadventures in Corporate Media*
Offers a fast-paced romp through the three major cable news channels—Fox CNN, and MSNBC—and delivers a serious message about their failure to cover the most urgent issues of the day.
$14.95, PAPERBACK.

STEVEN HILL, *10 Steps to Repair American Democracy*
Identifies the key problems with American democracy, especially election practices, and proposes ten specific reforms to reinvigorate it.
$11.00, PAPERBACK.

NOMI PRINS, *Jacked: How "Conservatives" Are Picking Your Pocket —Whether You Voted For Them or Not*
Describes how the "conservative" agenda has affected your wallet, skewed national priorities, and diminished America—but not the American spirit.
$12.00, PAPERBACK.

YVONNE LATTY, *In Conflict: Iraq War Veterans Speak Out on Duty, Loss, and the Fight to Stay Alive*
Features the unheard voices, extraordinary experiences, and personal photographs of a broad mix of Iraq War veterans, including Congressman Patrick Murphy, Tammy Duckworth, Kelly Daugherty, and Camilo Mejia.
$24.00, HARDCOVER.

JOHN SPERLING et al., *The Great Divide: Retro vs. Metro America*
Explains how and why our nation is so bitterly divided into what the authors call Retro and Metro America.
$19.95, PAPERBACK.

For more information, please visit www.p3books.com.